The Canoe Theory

Welcome to the team!

Tarat
Tom

The Canoe Theory

A Business Success Strategy for Leaders and Associates

Hibbard . Hibbard . Stockman, PhD

iUniverse, Inc.
Bloomington

The Canoe Theory
A Business Success Strategy for Leaders and Associates

iUniverse books may be ordered through booksellers or by contacting:

iUniverse
1663 Liberty Drive
Bloomington, IN 47403
www.iuniverse.com
1-800-Authors (1-800-288-4677)

ISBN: 978-0-595-36341-4 (pbk)
ISBN: 978-0-595-80778-9 (ebk)

Printed in the United States of America

iUniverse rev. date: 2/25/2011

The Canoe Theory

Think of your company
as a long canoe.

The canoe has a direction,
a destination.

Everyone has a seat and a paddle,
and everyone is expected to paddle.

Those who won't paddle
have to get out of the canoe.

Those who paddle well but
prevent others from paddling
have to adjust or get out of the canoe.

In times of personal crisis,
your compatriots will paddle for you.

You have the right to be happy.

THE MORAL OF THE CANOE THEORY

If you are going to be in the canoe,
then support the canoe or have
the integrity to leave rather
than stay and undermine
the canoe.

CONTENTS

ABOUT THE AUTHORS

David R. Hibbard

Born in Chicago and educated at Loyola University, David's corporate career began at Proctor & Gamble, where he developed the formal aspects of his leadership abilities. Prior to co-founding Dialexis, inc., Dave spent eighteen years in the highly competitive commercial real estate industry, where he developed impressive sales skills and street-smart savvy. He was honored as the "Number One Rookie" in the country, and the "Number One Broker" in one of the most aggressive real estate brokerage operations in the United States.

Later, as vice president at Grubb & Ellis, David transformed his office into one of the most profitable and respected brokerage operations in the nation using the principals of the Canoe Theory. He also became one of the leading trainers for all incoming Grubb & Ellis broker candidates. Grubb & Ellis is one of the nation's leading commercial real estate services firm, with offices in virtually every major metropolitan market in the United States. As a master trainer, Dave is recognized as one of the most progressive and intense instructors in the country. His approach is focused on getting individuals to the top 20%+ in all areas of life.

Today, David is a partner and acting CEO of the Dialexis organization. Dialexis has created innovative and original training solutions with a primary focus on mindset and tactics. Beginning with specific formulas for sales; The Soar Selling System™, a train-the-trainer program module incorporating twenty-five years of development yielding the most revolutionary approach to prospecting in the marketplace. This exclusive technology demonstrates "how to get appointments with decision makers," with national contact averages of 8 out of every 10 calls concluding with speaking to a decision maker or someone of high influence. In addition to the Dialexis sales methodology, the organization has also captivated leaders and staff with a team approach to leading people, ultimately increasing profits and employee satisfaction by enormous gains using the Canoe Theory Leadership methodology.

Marhnelle S. Hibbard

Marhnelle's background includes many years of experience as a certified corporate strategist. Prior to co-founding Dialexis, inc.™, Marhnelle enjoyed a successful fifteen-year career in the commercial real estate industry.

A highly regarded leadership and sales trainer, Marhnelle has the ability to affect

positive change in organizations undergo-
ing transition. Her hands-on coaching provides CEOs, managers, and leaders with
honest feedback, and offers effective and
innovative solutions for organizations and
individuals seeking execeptional results.

Marhnelle has advised and coached many
Fortune 500 and entrepreneurial organi-
zations such as Toshiba America, Irvine
Company, Gateway Computer, Herman
Miller, Countrywide Home Loans, Grubb &
Ellis, and DuPont.

Marhnelle believes in courageously taking on the real issues. Past clients attest
to the fact that she stands for creating
results.

Jack W. Stockman, PhD

Dr. Stockman has been a professor of
human resources at California State
University, Sacramento since 1970, and has
taught a variety of courses that focus on
the people dimension of organizations.

Dr. Stockman has taught in England and
France, and has consulted in Russia, Latvia,
and Turkmenistan of the former Soviet
Union. For the past decade, he taught
The Management of Contemporary
Organizations (OBE 150) through distance
learning. In the fall of 2000, he was invited

to China to consult with government and employee representatives on ESOP's and employee ownership.

Presently, he is a sought-after trainer, speaker, and management consultant in the areas of strategy development, change management, and all aspects of human concerns within organizations.

He has served on multiple local and national boards, including the Child Abuse Prevention Council, the Community Service Planning Council, and the Girl Scout Council. He is an active member of the Rotary Club.

Dr. Stockman earned his BA in psychology and management from Southern Illinois University and his PhD in organization theory and industrial relations at the University of Washington, Seattle.

Currently, Dr. Stockman is a principal consultant at Stockman and Associates, an organization focusing on strategic and human resources issues in private, public, and nonprofit organizations worldwide.

ACKNOWLEDGMENTS

The Canoe Theory™ is dedicated to all the individuals who have been courageous enough to share the truth, their experiences and their dedication to work toward positive change. We also want to thank the many people that have given of their time, vision, and encouragement to make this book a reality. Special thanks to Gabriel Nossovitch who has been a mentor, peer, and inspiration to so many. His vision of leadership and human potential is the essence of *The Canoe Theory*. Clint Crockett, who saw the magic of this philosophy and believed it had market potential; Karen DiFulgo, who saw the disconnect and has made it her work to reconnect; and Dr. Mark Goulston, author of multiple best-selling books, including *Getting Out of Your Own Way at Work...* and *Help Others Do the Same: Conquering Self-Defeating Behavior on the Job*. Mark has been such an amazing support. Scott Reinert, who is always pushing for excellence and stands for all the elements of The Canoe Theory; Don Turner, for providing the ultimate demonstration of how the Canoe Theory works.

Thanks also to Sandy Crabb, who as a leader knew there was more to the business side of business; Susana Grijalva, who stepped up to an editing challenge; Shelley Harriger, an amazing woman who constantly adds value in our work from editing this book to teaching the methodology; Annie McClinton, who was a spirit in developing the Canoe Theory into a leadership training program; Teri Millican, who is a constant and willing to do what it takes; Blair Mitchell, who has been the driving force in this entire process; Lynn Nelson, believed from the beginning; Karl Newman, the cheerleader; Katherine Schoettler, supported our Spanish version; and to all the people who have created positive change in the world by sharing and modeling the philosophy of the Canoe Theory.

And finally, a special thanks to our families, who make it all worthwhile.

INTRODUCTION

Knowing the corporation's strong reputation for exceptional sales accomplishments, clients from all sectors of the business community would request that Dialexis, inc.™ deliver sales seminars and training for both their sales and general staff. After delivering programs within many different companies and industries, it became obvious to the programs' trainers that the problems experienced by their clients weren't exclusively with the capabilities of the staff or sales groups but were, in fact, much more of a leadership malfunction.

For fifteen years, teams of individuals from Dialexis, inc.™ (formally Profit Techniques, Inc.) confidentially interviewed and conducted research to gather the opinions of thousands of employees and leaders in corporations throughout the United States. They discovered that approximately 87 percent of the organizations researched exhibited a disconnect between leaders and their teams.

The leaders believed the entire organization was dedicated to the goals of the organization—their goals—but the employees did not truly understand those goals. The leaders believed they were all headed "North" while the employees thought they were on their way "South"—therein lay the disconnect. The corporate goals the leaders worked to communicate to the employees were not being heard; therefore, the employees did not believe there was leadership within the organization. [1]

Simply stated, it appeared that few employees had a clear understanding of the direction, core values, or the urgent initiatives of their company.

When Dialexis delivered the results of its research, most managers were shocked with the answers provided by the employee rank and file. Most leaders were certain they had communicated where the organization was going and what the key initiatives were. Whether their efforts were ignored, their communication lacked clarity or focus, or their messages were, perhaps, simply not persuasive enough, the crucial connection had not been made. In fact, management was heading due north, while employees were heading due south.

To management's frustration, only the employees were aware of this disconnect. It seemed the employees could see that not everyone was on board with the direction of the organization. Through candid off line conversations, most of the employees were privy to how discontented a majority of the staff were—including some of the top performers in the company.

The Canoe Theory is a specific formula designed to help leaders create the missing connection within any organization, no matter the size, industry, or culture. Whether you are a leader, a staff member, or a new hire, you can make a significant difference in the performance and satisfaction of everyone in your organization.

This formula is made up of steps that leaders can follow to create a culture of teamwork and achievement. At the same time, the steps provide effective perspectives for the general population on how to "manage up," which is essential when helping to restructure your group or the entire organization. The simplicity of these steps will benefit everyone, and work will become more efficient, less frustrating, and potentially more fun than it's ever been.

In today's rapidly changing business climate, every organization needs to communicate a basic philosophy of core beliefs that shapes and governs individual and collective behavior. This philosophy becomes the organization's culture as it identifies the behaviors necessary to reach individual and enterprise potential. The staff of any organization is looking for its leaders to set the vision and course for the business—the canoe—so they can achieve the intended goals.

The Canoe Theory is a simple, yet powerful, set of principles that, when properly implemented, forms the foundation of high-performance companies. This theory has been applied in a multitude of organizations, large and small, with consistently profound results.

A canoe in motion is a fitting image for a successful business enterprise. The goal for the individuals in a company is, not simply to stay afloat but to arrive at the intended destination as efficiently as possible, using as few resources as necessary.

Furthermore, as anyone who's ever paddled a canoe will know, those aboard will only get to their common destination if they work in harmony, with each person's action complementing the actions of the others, while being careful not to take on too much water.

The goal of this book—and the principles it puts forth—are aimed at enhancing the working lives of both leaders and workers from all walks of the business world. The success of an organization is built upon the dual concepts of individual excellence and collective achievement. The synergistic consequences of this interaction are based upon three distinct factors—a positive attitude, a shared vision, and a commitment to team.

In order to be successful, every employee is expected to continuously ensure that his or her mix of behavior, attitude, skill, and experience will add value to the organization's overall mission. Everyone is responsible for his or her own employability. Longevity or loyalty is not sufficient to guarantee job security.

In return, each organization must be committed to offering challenging work, a supportive work culture, opportunities for growth and development, and a reward system that inspires performance.

The Canoe Theory is a metaphor for a contemporary organizational philosophy designed for the twenty-first century.

[1] Dialexis, inc.™ (formally Profit Techniques, Inc.)

THE CANOE THEORY: A LIFE APPLICATION

In November, my wife and I were invited by close friends, Scott and Jody to stay with them at their home in Hawaii. They had invited another couple Lisa and Brad, as well. The island and their home were beautiful, and their home was conveniently located next to a prominent hotel.

Given that our hosts had beach and hotel access, my wife and I along with our friends spent a good amount of time at the hotel beach enjoying sun, conversation, the sea, and hotel amenities. We snorkeled, swam, and played Bocce Ball on the beach. We noticed the hotel had three Hawaiian outrigger canoes at one end of the beach, waiting for tourists to learn the art of a long-standing cultural activity—long-canoe paddling, Hawaiian style. Over the next couple of days, we watched as various groups set out in the outriggers, always returning laughing and seemingly energized. It wasn't long before Scott our host said, "Does anyone want to take one of those canoe rides?" The answer was a resounding, "Yes!"

We scheduled reservations for 8 AM the next day. We were greeted by our lead instructor and one of his teammates. The lead instructor was friendly but seemed pretty intense for a guy who appeared to have a pretty enjoyable job. Don't get me wrong: he was polite, but he didn't seem to be in a jovial mood as we were—he was nice but definitely serious.

The canoe was sitting on the sand a good 50 feet from the ocean's edge, and I noticed as we approached that it was much larger than it seemed from a distance. It was big enough to hold all six of us plus the two instructors.

After a meet-and-greet session, the lead instructor began by asking for our attention—it was apparent he was in charge. He wasn't rude, but he certainly wanted us to listen—and we listened. He began by telling us about the components of the canoe. He described the paddles, the seats, and the general concept of Hawaiian paddling—the overall intent of what we were about to do. I remember thinking that it seemed like overkill for instruction. After all, how hard can paddling be? I just wanted to get out there and have a few laughs. I couldn't figure out why this guy was so serious.

Once he completed his initial introduction, we were all ready to get going. I thought, "now we're going to launch and have some fun," but that isn't what happened. Instead, this guy became intent on informing us in exact detail how we needed to conduct ourselves in the canoe. Next, he requested that each of us take a seat in the canoe—not just any seat, but particular seats. He obviously wanted us seated in a manner that would benefit the movement of the canoe and support each paddler's attributes. After all, we had three men and three women, all of different sizes, weights, and strength. He placed each person in the canoe in a location that would provide balance, power, and safety. It was becoming apparent that this wasn't just a canoe ride to him—this was a cultural experience based on history and deep respect for the Hawaiian way.

Once we were all seated, he explained exactly how to put our paddles in the water for maximum power delivery—despite the fact that the canoe was still sitting in the sand. He told us how to support one another and how to use every ability we each had for a mutual result. He taught us the verbal commands that he would be calling out during our activity, which were his signals in the Hawaiian language indicating when to dig the paddle in, when to lift it, when to stop, and so on. He made sure we could repeat the terms in unison and asked us to yell out the words after him until he was certain that we got it. It seemed somewhat strange to me at first. I thought, "Let's just get going. Why do we have to spend so much time on all this detail? It's just a canoe ride!"

Finally, the instructor said, "Okay, let's get the canoe in the water." It was clear that he was satisfied that we were prepared to succeed as a team. At that point, my respect for him and his leadership began to awaken. I respected his discipline and his obvious commitment to our success. I began to shift my mindset.

As a team, we pushed and pulled our canoe to the water's edge. It took all of our strength. Once the canoe was afloat, we took our positions as instructed, holding our paddles exactly as we had been told and sitting upright ready to move our canoe forward as a team. I remember feeling well prepared, wanting to please our instructor and do my part as a committed team member. After all, he was at the back of the canoe and able to watch my competency. I didn't want to disappoint him or my other team members—I felt an obligation to perform to his standards.

Once we were past the wave break, he informed us of our intended direction and then loudly shouted out his first command in his native Hawaiian language: "Ho-mau-kau-kau" (Are you ready?), then his second command, "Hoe-ai-api" (Lift the paddle), then his third command, "Imua" (Paddle in the water), and then "Hut! Ho!" (Change your paddle from the right to the left or from the left to the right of the canoe). Suddenly, we were operating as a team as we dug our paddles into the water, maximizing our task. The canoe started cutting through the Pacific Ocean.

I was third from the front, and I was doing exactly what my compatriots were doing—giving it my all. I was focused on Scott our lead paddler in the bow of the canoe; matching his every move, his timing, and the depth his paddle entered the water. We were all following him—just as we had been trained to do.

Our instructor moved through the commands precisely as he had told us he would, and we were responsive to his every call—we had been well trained and it showed. Once we got to our destination, he called out

"Lawa," his command to stop—and we did. As the canoe slowed and we floated above crystal clear water, admiring the beauty of Hawaii, he complemented us as a team. I was pleased that he was pleased, and I was proud of our team—I was also proud of myself.

We saw turtles and coral, and we absorbed the moment sitting still in the water. After we enjoyed our initial effort to reach our destination, he instructed us to head back.

We turned the canoe and again followed his commands; the paddling was now getting tiring and took all we had to maintain our consistency. As we neared the beach—approximately two hundred yards from completing our trip—our instructor began to increase the intensity of the task.

He asked us to really move the canoe. He bellowed out his commands powerfully, encouraging us to give everything—and we did. Despite the fact that the sun was intense, we became amazing as a team: no misses, pure unison, everyone digging deep. It was fantastic. Even members of the team began to yell, "Dig, dig!" We started flying—really flying—with no errors, just focused commitment. We moved that canoe with eight people on board at breakneck speed toward the beach. Our instructor never stopped encouraging us with his powerful voice: "Go, go! Dig, dig!" Suddenly, we heard him yell, "Lawa!" and we stopped— exhausted, wet, hot, and proud of what we did as a team.

Everyone had given 100 percent on our final effort to the beach—no whining, no stopping, no excuses … just driven team commitment. It was exhilarating. We cheered; we congratulated one another and thanked our leader—everyone was beaming. We had just accomplished something much bigger than a canoe ride.

The next day I thought back, mentally reviewing how I had initially approached the canoe on the beach. I then realized that I had been

xxiv The Canoe Theory

walking toward that canoe with my own agenda in mind, but powerful leadership shifted my mindset. Our leader had been serious. He was committed to our growth—to the experience he wanted us to learn—and it wasn't just about paddling a canoe; it was about achievement, life, and the power of a team. Through strong leadership, my doubts, judgments, and preconceived notions had been erased, and in many ways, I was more bonded with my team than I had been one hour prior to our launch. We were now bonded through a sense of accomplishment and mutual effort. A level of appreciation and respect for one another was instilled.

Final Comment

Despite being one of the authors of The Canoe Theory and believing in its philosophy and its value to individuals and organizations, I now realize that applying the Canoe Theory in other areas of life besides business works as well, and when it does, it's truly a powerful experience.

David Hibbard

" Okay, Let's get the
canoe in the water. "

TWO CASE STUDIES

Company "A"

Several years ago, the president of a real estate property management group discovered there was a disconnect between the perceptions of his company's goals by employees and the perceptions by management, despite the fact that the organization was considered best in class based on indicators such as growth, profits, and acknowledgments from industry peers.

The president envisioned that if all segments of his organization were truly connected and that if his people were focused on supporting one another as a team, there would be no limit to what could be accomplished.

The customers would benefit, and the employees and management alike would love working there. The company would suffer less attrition, attract top talent, and measurably increase profit.

Even though his organization employed more than 650 people at the time, the president committed himself to creating this environment and making a difference in each of his employees' lives.

Working closely with his management team, he developed several internal groups to focus on issues key to realigning the culture of his company, such as communication and employee appreciation.

However, a year went by, and despite his intentions and efforts, the president came to terms with the reality that he and his team were not breaking through to the real issues.

On the surface it seemed they were making progress, but behind the scenes it was a completely different scenario. There were some people within the organization that did not want a cohesive team. They felt most powerful when the staff didn't communicate their honest thoughts or feelings. So at times there were duel conversations going on. One conversation to managers and another to co-workers. As an example, one day the leasing managers were asked to review the follow up status of their leasing staff. In the meeting the leasing managers said "everything is fine, everyone is following up and progress is being made".

After the meeting the true feelings were shared, "Who do they think they are to check up on me—management doesn't know how busy we are" and it got worse. The managers felt they were being checked up on or micro managed. The leasing managers didn't trust their managers to share the truth. And some of the leasing managers enjoyed exchanging gossip rather than have an honest conversation. This type of gossip and negative, destructive conversations were taking place daily to the point that it was beginning to undermine the president's vision.

Resolution

The president was not a stranger to adversity, and he was determined to see his vision become a reality. As an effective leader, he knew he needed help shifting the organization. And to do so, he decided to call a respected consultant for support.

The first conversation between the president and the consultant uncovered the president's realization that although he had been a successful manager and leader for many years, in order to see new or shifted results, he would first need to adjust his leadership style.

The president accepted the personal challenge to shift his leadership style, and as a result, he became even more committed to his vision. Which, forever altered the destination of his company.

Over the next few months, the consultant introduced the president and his management team to a leadership concept called the Canoe Theory. They held meetings on how to motivate employees and keep them in the canoe. The goal was to rally the entire workforce into this new culture of people serving people.

Two and a half months later, the president brought together his entire organization to roll out the new vision.

A translator was brought in so the non-English members—from the maintenance manager to the day porter to leasing consultants—understood the company's new direction.

As the Canoe Theory was implemented—by holding daily, weekly, and monthly training sessions; reviewing new expectations; rewarding new behaviors; and taking a myriad of other actions—the president and his management team grew stronger and more effective. They understood the need to support and coach their employees as teammates, while at the same time holding them accountable to the new standards.

Today, this organization lives by the tenets of the Canoe Theory, and as they grow and continue to work through their issues, they stand together with honesty, with accountability, and with open dialogue.

Their mantra is, "People serving people."

A national business journal publication named Company "A" one of the best places to work in the country.

During recent economic shifts, Company "A" responded with urgency as a united front and minimized the effects of potentially negative market conditions. The results were impressive:

* Personal performance increased
* Attrition went down by 40 percent
* All industry indicators (occupancy, rents, etc.) were at the top of the market

This company is a living example of the Canoe Theory at work—with well over 1,000 individuals paddling together.

Company "B"

In San Francisco, California, two very successful companies merged, creating a nightmare for both management and employees. One company was very process-driven, and the other company was very sales/marketing-driven.

This created a challenge. However, the two new owners were already adept at handling people issues and communicating with each other since they had already been trained in, and had made a commitment to, the basic premise of the Canoe Theory.

Knowing that the accomplishment of their shared goals depended on cooperation, the owners implemented weekly and monthly meetings with teams from both prior companies to smooth the transition and create a new company culture that embraced the Canoe Theory as part of day-to-day operations.

The owners of the previous companies authentically believed in the potential of the Canoe Theory. Their employees saw this, and because of their respect and belief in the owners' leadership, they took this new idea to heart. Each day the challenges seemed to be fewer, and business really began to expand. New and existing customers became comfortable with the merger, and everything seemed to be going in the right direction.

The company was operating at maximum capacity with existing staff. The entire organization was under tremendous pressure because of this new growth, and everyone was working 60-plus hours a week to keep up with the demands and the pace of the business.

As management frantically began searching for new talent to support their team, they became aware of the "power down" methods of one particular division leader.

As pressure to keep up with the additional workload increased, Mark, the division leader in question, became more and more stressed. He began abusing his power and belittling his people by yelling at, making demands on, and demoralizing anyone under his authority.

Mark had an outstanding record of productivity and customer satisfaction. So, at first, the owners tried to rationalize his behavior and requested he adjust his style of interaction with his people. But his behavior continued to be demeaning and aggressive, so they knew they had to take action.

Resolution

The owners felt backed into a corner. Yet they understood the principles of Tenet #5 of the Canoe Theory: those who paddle well but prevent others from paddling have to adjust or get out of the canoe.

Key leaders held numerous coaching conversations with Mark, suggesting he adapt his behavior to support his team. Emphasizing their shared goals, the leaders stressed the importance of team-building and creating an inclusive—not exclusive—environment.

Ultimately, Mark responded that it was "his way or the highway." He was not willing to change his leadership style or his attitude. He believed getting the work done was all that mattered.

After difficult consideration, the management team decided that Mark had to be released. This was a difficult decision since his results in getting the job done and receiving customer endorsements put him among the industry's best. Nevertheless, management believed a commitment to the Canoe Theory was the foundation for their future.

Following Mark's release, a new division leader who had worked under Mark was promoted from within the department, but sadly, the damage Mark had done was significant. As division head, Mark had been the role model for his department. After a few weeks, management discovered that the new division leader had formed the same destructive habits as Mark, and they asked him to resign.

Eventually, it became apparent that the poison had gone three levels deep. Mark, the succeeding division manager, and the following manager, all had the same disparaging style.

Despite these challenges, the leadership remained upbeat about their potential to affect positive change among both employees and management. And once everyone understood that both a positive attitude and positive performance were required to remain employed, a new leader was selected from within the division and became successful.

Team members learned that being respectful of one another is a core value of the Canoe Theory, and the entire organization is flourished once again.

ATTITUDE + PERFORMANCE = EMPLOYABILITY

PART
one

The Canoe Theory: A True Story

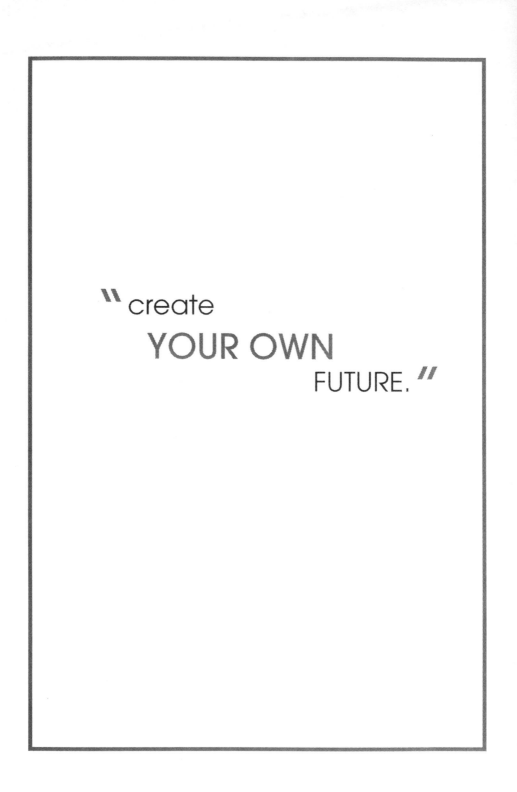

" create
YOUR OWN
FUTURE. "

Part One
The Canoe Theory: A True Story

It was a rainy, overcast day in early spring when Jeff Allen, owner and CEO of Glassco Production Industries, began to think about the future of his organization.

He had been involved with Glassco in many capacities over his fifteen years. He had been hired originally for a sales position, and he had never thought he would become an owner in the equipment manufacturing industry.

Jeff worked his way up from new business development representative to sales manager, to president and general manager. Last year, Jeff purchased the business from several partners and became the sole owner.

Glassco had its share of successes and challenges. There were times when new engineering projects in San Francisco, Washington, and Hawaii created very profitable results. There were also economic downturns when sales were down, and pay cuts and layoffs were the order of the day.

Overall, Glassco's reputation and image were extremely positive. The business had gained attention for its innovative engineering design work, and its manufacturing practices were seen by most as the best in the industry.

It was not the present or the past, however, that occupied Jeff's thoughts that day, but the future. In his heart, Jeff felt it would soon be time for a major change in his life. He had begun to think about an exit strategy for himself and how that might affect the future of Glassco. He had spent fifteen years of his life building the organization, and it was important to him that his legacy of positive leadership continues after he left.

The most obvious option would be to sell. That would mean finding an outside party who could purchase the assets and inherit the company's goodwill, but would an outsider understand and preserve the spirit of the company he had worked so hard to create?

Over the previous four years, Jeff had assembled a work group of over seventy-five industrial engineers, customer support representatives, and sales professionals, most of whom were extremely competent, committed, and loyal to him and to Glassco.

Many of these people had been with the company since he started. His concern was that new owners might not retain this talented group of people and might dismantle what he had worked so hard to create.

Jeff was also concerned for the welfare of his employees and for the continued success of the organization he had built. Glassco had thrived in part because Jeff's employees knew that he genuinely was committed to their well-being, and their appreciation was reflected in their pursuit of success.

At a conference he had attended some months before, one of the speakers proposed an Employee Stock Ownership Plan (ESOP) as a strategy for transferring ownership of an organization.

An ESOP allows employees to purchase the firm from the owner, and in turn become the owners themselves. The concept had a great deal of appeal for Jeff, so he decided to learn more about the details.

After six months of meetings with accountants, tax specialists, and attorneys, Jeff concluded that pursing an ESOP would best suit his goals, the employees' goals, and the future of Glassco.

Working together, he and his team of consultants developed a plan. His employees would own the company in just five years, and Jeff would be free to pursue other ventures.

However, there was a challenge Jeff had to conquer before he could feel comfortable about the future. He had to have confidence that the management team succeeding him would have the same level of commitment and dedication that he had held for the company.

Jeff spent many hours thinking about the foundation of Glassco, its values, what it stood for, and what made it such a successful organization. He wanted to come up with a plan that would pass on his leadership strategy to the new Glassco employees and leaders.

Jeff knew that an organization built on the dual concepts of individual excellence and collective achievement was a key issue. This collective synergy would be based on three critical factors:

* A positive attitude
* A shared vision
* A commitment to team

Each of these principles had been a major factor behind Glassco's success, and Jeff was convinced that these notions needed to be carried forward by the employees to ensure the company's future success.

Furthermore, he realized that in order to achieve success, every associate of Glassco would need to continuously develop his or her mix of behavior, attitude, skill, and experience in order to add value to the mission of the organization.

He knew that each employee was responsible for his or her own employ-ability and longevity, and that seniority alone would not guarantee future job security.

Most importantly, Jeff knew that Glassco could offer each of the future owners a unique opportunity for success. If they could continue to work together and reach the firm's potential, the employees would enjoy eco-nomic rewards and personal satisfaction beyond their wildest dreams.

As a leader, Jeff firmly believed that if he could develop a philoso-phy—a culture that captured the essence of Glassco, one that would serve as a guide for all employees/owners to follow—he could create something that would forever influence the destiny of Glassco. He also understood that such a philosophy would be applicable to any organi-zation—private, public, or nonprofit.

All Jeff could think about for the next several weeks were the funda-mental philosophies that strengthen what he wanted to instill in each of Glassco's employees.

Coincidentally, Jeff had recently returned from an industry conference where he had listened to a speaker share concepts similar to the legacy he wanted to create for Glassco which was called the Canoe Theory.

Jeff realized the company had many of the Canoe Theory tenets in place but didn't have a clear, articulated philosophy. He knew the Canoe Theory would allow him to do that.

These concepts were explained as a leadership principle called the Canoe Theory. Jeff was inspired, and immediately began formulating a plan to implement the ideas he had heard.

"Individual commitment to a group effort—that is what makes a team work, a company work, a society work, a civilization work."

<u>Vince Lombardi</u>
US football coach (1913–1970)
Coach of Green Bay Packers 1959–1967
Coach of Washington Redskins 1969

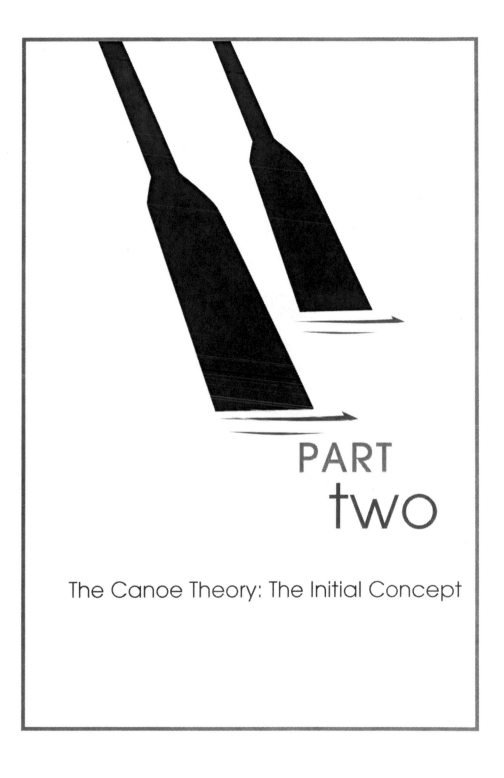

PART
two

The Canoe Theory: The Initial Concept

TENET 1:
THINK OF
YOUR COMPANY
AS A LONG CANOE

Jeff began by dissecting each tenet of the Canoe Theory. He knew that for the future owners of Glassco Production Industries to succeed, they would all have to work together and see themselves in the same canoe.

From his experience leading Glassco, Jeff understood that thinking of a successful, thriving business as a canoe made a lot of sense. Unlike the skills of drivers of automobiles, the ability of a canoe's occupants to get to their shared destination depends fully on their synchronicity and cooperation. Harmony of action, not the independent pursuit of self-fulfillment, brings success in both canoeing and business. And Jeff knew that the path of a canoe's travel—the water—could often be just as tumultuous and unpredictable as a business's path to success.

Over the years, a distinguished culture had been created under Jeff's leadership, and he believed that culture was at the core of Glassco's success. Most employees demonstrated their commitment to this culture through their behaviors and attitudes that supported functioning as a team. There was an understanding that everyone was connected to the results and that responsibilities were universal—meaning everyone accepted accountability for the success of the end product and the service that Glassco delivered to its clients.

Jeff recalled that when he first joined Glassco, there was no team. It felt more like twelve strangers. No communication, no solid meetings about the strategy for Glassco—just do your job and move through the day. Jeff realized quickly that this was not the way to really succeed. His peers were more like crafty competitors. It was a very win-lose mentality—yet, he had always believed that if they had been more collaborative, Glassco could have been much farther ahead of the real competition and everyone would realize more success.

When Jeff became the sole owner of the company, he was committed to bringing everyone together as a team and creating a more collaborative environment—one that fostered sharing, exchanging ideas, building strategies together, and being competitive and exciting, but not cutthroat or following a path where "you win" meant "I lose." The new environment of trust, communication, and team was at the core of the new culture. It was very different from the existing culture, but Jeff was confident this new culture would set Glassco in a new direction.

Reflecting on those past years, Jeff felt proud of what he had created. This unique culture based on functioning as a whole had been established over many years—a culture that truly defined the way Glassco conducted business, brought in clients, and supported their employees. This specific set of rules and values was at the very heart of the business. He also realized from being in the industry for many years that most of his competitors' cultures were extremely different.

One competent competitor frequently lost business to Glassco because this company repeatedly missed deadlines. Their culture was so focused on their technical excellence and creativity that deadlines weren't kept and were considered unimportant.

Another competitor was timely and creative, but the culture was focused solely on being creative and meeting deadlines; as a result, managers and employees did not appreciate or embrace people from their internal staff, and their clients thought they were rude and arrogant. Jeff was proud of the balance he had created with his team at Glassco—being timely, technical, and creative mattered, but so did positive client interaction and staff appreciation.

Glassco's culture attracted top talent and made the company different from their competitors. It allowed Glassco to be the leader in the field and stay at the forefront of the industry.

Jeff was concerned that if he were no longer at the helm, others might not understand or maintain this corporate philosophy. He believed that for the organization to continue to grow and succeed, employees at all levels needed to actively pursue success and quality in their work. Each employee should be responsible and accountable for their performance, and for the performance of others.

Remembering the metaphor of a canoe, Jeff knew that interdependence among all employees was essential. Glassco would not survive if, individually and collectively, everyone were not in the canoe.

Jeff understood how powerful it would be if everyone were focused on the same objectives and understood that actively working together was the key to success. A shared vision would provide a collective direction and purpose.

Jeff realized this was a key component of The Canoe Theory. He understood that by sharing his vision with everyone at Glassco, he would preserve the legacy and traditions of the company. He was ready for the second tenet of The Canoe Theory.

"**Trust** men and
they will be **true** to you;
treat them greatly, and they
will show themselves **great**. "

Ralph Waldo Emerson
American Author, Poet & Philosopher (1803–1882)
Essays, First Series: Prudence, 1841

TENET 2:

THE CANOE HAS A DIRECTION, A DESTINATION

What could be more powerful than a shared vision—a future everyone can support and become enthusiastic about?

Jeff knew if he could communicate to everyone a challenging yet achievable vision for their future—a crusade of sorts—they could get the canoe moving in a more exciting direction. He understood that if individuals have the opportunity to have a voice in the development of the vision, they will have moved from being a mission-statement-driven organization to an organization with a real mission—a team-driven plan for action.

He realized that his employees must understand and believe in the mission or core purpose of Glassco in order to secure maximum commitment, and the specific nature of positioning their vision as a crusade meant to Jeff that his people would pull together to accomplish a purpose with energy, similar to a campaign or a movement. Jeff knew this was a powerful distinction for Glassco.

Jeff also knew that everyone must have the opportunity to contribute for their ideas and help develop the vision, because the people who inherited this vision would be around long after Jeff was gone. This meant good communication was essential at all levels and in all directions. Complete buy-in was critical.

Goals, objectives, activities, and tasks must all flow from the mission and vision of the organization, which would guide the canoe to an exciting future.

Jeff began to reflect on how he might achieve this shared vision and how that shared vision could be translated into a crusade.

Every individual at Glassco needed to embrace the same passion and commitment in order to create a future for the organization and for themselves. Their ideas were critical to determining the direction the company would follow. Jeff would need to reach out and solicit the ideas and thoughts of his employees about what they believed should be the direction of Glassco so that he would have the fullest understanding of his legacy's potential.

As he thought about the metaphor of a long canoe with a direction for Glassco, Jeff realized that for the organization to be successful, everyone in the canoe would have to have a place from which to operate.

Once this was accomplished, Jeff would be ready to implement the third tenet of The Canoe Theory.

TENET 3:

EVERYONE HAS A SEAT

AND A PADDLE,

AND EVERYONE

IS EXPECTED TO PADDLE

Jeff called a meeting of all his senior managers and told them he needed their help craft the direction of Glassco. It took the team most of the day on the white board, throwing out ideas and possibilities for what Glassco's future looked like and the potential that it had in today's marketplace. At the end of the day they felt good about the work they had accomplished. Next they set up a meeting where everyone on the payroll was in attendance. At that meeting the senior management team rolled out their thoughts on what the direction of Glassco should be, and then they asked their people for their thoughts. They broke into small groups to discuss what the management team had presented and then each group gave feedback and refined the original ideas for the direction of Glassco. Jeff thought it was interesting watching some reactions from the associates.

This was the first time the entire team had gotten together to chart out the course of where Glassco was headed. By the end of the meeting, almost 3 hours had gone by, everyone was excited. Jeff could feel the energy in the room. There was a true sense of connection that was beginning and it felt good. Jeff was astute to the fact that if Glassco was going to be successful, it was going to take everyone's commitment to the challenge and new direction and after that meeting, he felt confident Glassco was on its way.

Now that the vision of Glassco had been established, its vision could never be realized unless every associate fulfilled the expectations associated with their particular function and responsibilities.

It was not enough just to be in the canoe. Every individual must clearly understand the roles they would play, the activities for which they would be responsible, and how they would be held accountable.

Jeff understood that roles and responsibilities are the seats and the paddles of an organization. If everyone were to execute their duties flawlessly, and in sync with each other's efforts, the canoe would move steadily forward. This was a significant point, and emphasized why implementing the Canoe Theory philosophy was so appropriate for the future of Glassco.

Jeff made a mental note to connect compensation to this theme. It seemed logical that salaries, bonuses, and commissions should be directly related to how well each associate performed his or her roles and responsibilities. While he knew that the equal cooperation of all employees was vital to arriving at their shared destination, he also understood the power of positive reinforcement through compensation.

One morning Jeff arrived at Glassco and found Irene (not one of his best employees) surfing the Web at her desk.

Jeff knew that Irene was there to get a rush order processed, but it was obvious that nothing productive was happening at Irene's desk.

It was just what the third tenet of the Canoe Theory stressed: you can't just sit in the canoe; you have to paddle. As he thought more about Irene, it crystallized his idea that Glassco would reach its goal, but not without the power and timeliness of a team effort where everyone paddled. Jeff knew this was the key to exceptional achievement.

There was a key manager Jeff knew he could trust and rely on to perform at the highest level; her name was Carol. She was in charge of technical design and had been with Jeff a long time. When he compared Irene to Carol, Jeff realized that he spent more time and energy managing Irene than he did mentoring Carol. He saw in Carol that both attitude and performance were essential to a person meeting and exceeding their dreams and goals. Jeff reasoned that the canoe would glide even more effectively toward its goals if these were the expectations for everyone.

He concluded that he needed to adjust his expectations of Irene and others. He focused on the formula A + P = E and found that it must be his measuring stick for potential employment at Glassco.

Attitude + Performance = Employability.

This formula led Jeff to think about Tenet #4 of the Canoe Theory.

"Employability means you control your own future and choose to continually improve your value to the corporation. Associates challenge their employer to insure they are growing and enhancing their "employability." Corporations that insure their associates are "employable as best in class" remain vital. Corporations expand their investment in divisions and in associates that are constantly adding value and generating future returns. A + P = E (Attitude + Performance = Employability)."

Tim Baucom
VP-Marketing; Shaw Commercial Division
Shaw Industries, a Berkshire Hathaway subsidiary
A business professional recognizing the importance of leadership

TENET 4:
THOSE WHO
WON'T PADDLE HAVE TO
GET OUT OF THE CANOE

A few weeks passed before Jeff could solidify his thoughts regarding this principle. Jeff drew upon examples within his own sales division where the performance of senior sales professionals had dropped off from the early years, despite many of these individuals being loyal, long-term employees.

These individuals had been top performers at one point, but, because of market conditions, they began to lose key accounts. This can, and does, happen to sales professionals in any industry. But what compounded the problem at Glassco was that after the accounts dropped off, the sales reps' efforts to capture new accounts became sluggish at best.

When management questioned the lack of new business, the sales reps would tell their stories and provide excuses for why business wasn't happening. These well-articulated excuses began to add up, and Jeff recalled thinking that for the reps to remain employed, loyalty could not be the only deciding factor. It wouldn't be enough to merely want to make more sales; remaining at Glassco would depend on results—and on the quality and outcome of their efforts. If they didn't develop new accounts, they couldn't be part of this team.

The canoe needed everyone to contribute with their maximum capabilities in order to be successful. Jeff instinctively believed these salespeople did have the capacity to identify and close new business, but it was their attitude or complacency that was the issue. He saw that Glassco did not have the resources to allow these individuals to be in the canoe and not paddle. Jeff also realized he needed to investigate to find out whether nonpaddling, or nonperformance, was because of attitude or lack of skill. Did some of his people require more training or mentoring?

At that moment, Jeff remembered seeing Irene surfing the Web. He had certainly spent time training Irene, but had he really given her the guidelines for success? The bottom line was that it was his responsibility to outline the expectations for each member of each group and make certain they had the tools to be successful. Glassco needed everyone to contribute to their fullest. Everyone needed to produce results in order to stay in the canoe.

It would also be imperative that every person in the canoe create the results they had been hired to produce, no matter which division they worked for.

Jeff grabbed his organizer and wrote a reminder to himself: if they don't paddle, they have to get out of the canoe. Excuses won't make it anymore.

As he wrote, he articulated what would become a core element to the future success of Glassco. And as Jeff reflected on past highs and lows within the company, he began to fully understand this important premise of leadership from the Canoe Theory:

Loyalty + A Well-Articulated Excuse ≠ (does not equal) Employment

"Make up your mind to act decidedly and take the consequences. No good is ever done in this world by hesitation. "

Thomas H. Huxley
English biologist (1825–1895)
Author of *Man's Place in Nature*

TENET 5:

THOSE WHO PADDLE WELL BUT PREVENT OTHERS

FROM PADDLING HAVE TO

ADJUST OR GET OUT

OF THE CANOE

the Canoe Theory was finally beginning to come together. But the reality of holding his top performers to the same standards as all Glassco employees was going to be the most difficult tenet to embrace. There had been times—many times—when Jeff knew he had looked the other way when it came to his top achievers. He recalled the time a quarterly report was due. This was a deadline Jeff was adamant about being met. Nonetheless, once again he had allowed Craig, his top engineer, another week to turn in his report. Jeff had made allowances for several top performers, and, with a sinking feeling, he knew this would have to stop … beginning now. Why had Jeff created such different rules and expectations for the top performers? He knew exactly why: he had fallen into the notion that top performers were a special breed, and that special breeds needed to have the mundane taken out of their lives.

The more Jeff thought about his behavior, the worse he felt. He had really let his organization down. Everyone needed to contribute, especially his top employees.

Jeff knew that the ultimate success of Glassco would depend on everyone in the organization pulling together to blend their diverse talents and to work as a team.

He also knew that the attitude and behavior of all the company's employees would be the real key to long-term growth and achievement.

Jeff recognized that no single individual should be allowed to hamper the success of the canoe in reaching its destination, and that the part could not be as important as the whole.

He understood that some employees were exceptional performers, and as a result, they were essential to the output of the organization. In fact, if they were truly exceptional performers, they should be able to be counted on even more in a team-leader capacity. They should be thought of and respected as the best—therefore, they should not be shortcutting the process or needing extensions, but rather they should be the first ones to hand in their reports or have the most complete paperwork without pushing their work onto others.

He especially realized that even though certain individuals performed exceptionally well, there could be no exceptions for prima donna performers.

One employee fitting this description was Rick. Although an exceptional technical designer, he was always late for meetings. Sometimes, he wouldn't return his colleagues' phone calls for days. By behaving in these ways, Rick was definitely not supporting his co-workers or the organization effectively.

In order for Glassco to reach—and remain at—the apex of success, everyone would be required to maintain a supportive and cooperative environment despite different levels of achievement.

Once again, Jeff thought the whole must not suffer because of the part. He was committed to reestablishing the guidelines for his entire team—everyone must adhere to the process and expectations of Glassco because it was going to take everyone's contribution to consistently succeed.

With that new awareness, Jeff also was beginning to consider how Glassco could be more compassionate toward the team members. Jeff knew that when economic markets shifted, Glassco would face unforeseen challenges, and everyone would be needed to respond to future challenges.

And yet these challenges might cause Glassco to alter its course or adopt new strategies. Jeff realized that this kind of change likely would cause stress and anxiety for everyone, and Jeff needed his people to adjust to the company's crises and challenges.

He also understood that in life there are unforeseen circumstances that may cause disruptions in personal lives, such as illness, divorce, or any number of difficulties. It was critical that the organization and all the individuals involved have an understanding, a philosophy, and a systematic approach to deal with such realities. Jeff knew the whole must not suffer because of the part, but he also compassionately understood that the whole must never let the part suffer.

As he thought more about this, Jeff began to understand why the next tenet of the Canoe Theory made so much sense: the organization must be prepared to support a team member in need; in times of personal crisis, your compatriots will paddle for you.

" One man can be a crucial ingredient on a team, but one man cannot make a team. **"**

Kareem Abdul Jabbar,
Los Angeles Lakers; Creator of the Sky-Hook
Hall of Fame NBA Center

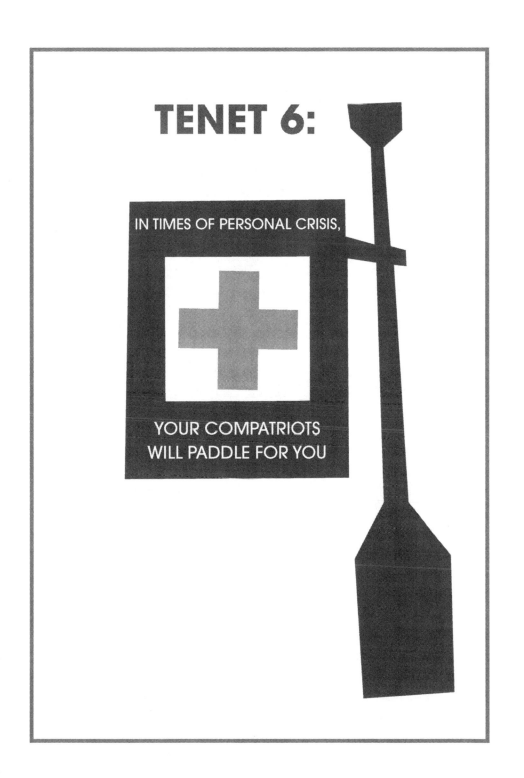

A valued associate who experiences stress or personal crisis that hinders their potential, or the team's potential, must be nurtured and supported by the organization, using appropriate strategies for intervention when necessary.

The practical application of the Canoe Theory is based on the notion of TEAM (Together Everyone Achieves More), which includes assisting associates when a personal crisis occurs.

Jeff acknowledged that just as at any company, Glassco employees would likely face many crises in the coming years, and that everyone would be tested by their ability to pull together and meet those challenges.

Everyone needed to understand how to support a colleague in need. Each individual needed to know that if a team member faced a significant crisis in his or her life, this person could, for a reasonable amount of time, put down their paddle and all his or her teammates would pick up the slack.

This was a critical key to building a sustainable organization—people serving and supporting each other.

Jeff realized that the rate of change in his industry was relentless. As he had learned in his years at Glassco, pressure would be part of day-to-day business, and this seemed to apply as far into the future as Jeff could see. Every associate must be in the canoe with complete focus; anything less than a focused effort would not be acceptable.

However, Jeff was a realist and knew from his experience of being part of Glassco for the past fifteen years that personal crises were inevitable, just as corporate difficulties were. He understood that personal crises would be best supported by each individual's effort to pick up the slack when a member needed support.

The organization Jeff envisioned for his associates would be dedicated to the success of every individual in the Glassco canoe. Jeff realized this was at the very core of his belief. He knew that if Glassco could support its people when they needed it, the people would be more likely to support Glassco in its time of need. This was the defining moment as Jeff was gaining clarity about the power of the Canoe Theory's principles.

Yet there was still something in the back of Jeff's mind. Notwithstanding a personal crisis, everyone who chose to be in the canoe must perform at a superior level—despite the sort of mundane difficulties all individuals face.

If employees chose to behave inappropriately, either by not playing team ball, or not supporting the canoe in the manner dictated by the philosophy of the Canoe Theory, they would jeopardize their team and themselves, which brought Jeff to the next tenet: everyone had to decide if they wanted to be in the canoe, and ultimately it was their choice.

TENET 7:
YOU HAVE THE RIGHT TO
BE HAPPY

A powerful release of energy came over Jeff as he thought about Tenet #7. He realized that if any troubled individuals continued to put themselves at risk in the canoe, they just couldn't be happy.

This made so much sense to Jeff. From his own experiences, he knew a happy employee would never participate in self-sabotage.

Jeff was puzzled by the idea that an individual who had the ability to paddle well just wouldn't. Anyone who would interfere with others, be uncooperative, or under perform would essentially be sabotaging the future of their own employment.

As a positive person, he decided that the final concept of the Canoe Theory supported all employees: everyone has the right to be happy.

If an employee didn't like where the canoe was going, who was in the canoe, where he or she was sitting, the paddle, or any other condition, that employee had the right to seek a positive resolution. Sometimes this would be possible in the canoe, and sometimes it wouldn't. If the employee couldn't arrive at an understanding or get behind and support the canoe, the canoe would simply pull over to shore and let the employee out to get into a canoe he or she did like.

With so many canoes, so many destinations, so many cultures, and so many choices, why would an individual stay in a canoe that made him or her unhappy? Jeff realized that just because employees were unhappy, or discovered that they were in a canoe that didn't suit their interests; it shouldn't create a negative response from management.

If management really cared about every single individual, management should support a person in leaving the canoe so he or she could ultimately be happy—and the canoe could continue smoothly on its way. Jeff thought to himself this was the win-win he had always wanted to create in the culture of Glassco, and now he realized he had a true understanding of how to support both the company and his people.

As Jeff reflected on his years at Glassco and the ideas he'd recently been distilling from his experiences, he was impressed both by the simplicity and by the complexity of this new philosophy.

He had articulated it in his mind and personalized it with his vision. Now he was ready to integrate it into Glassco.

The first step would be to have a meeting with employees to ask for their thoughts, ideas, concerns, and hopes for the future of the company. Once this was done, Jeff would synthesize all the input and create a road map for Glassco. After completing this task, Jeff would bring the entire company together to communicate the direction of the canoe, requesting that every individual decide if this was the right canoe for him or her.

But before he would ask for everyone's commitment, there needed to be some of what Jeff had come to think of as emotional cleanup. Jeff would begin this process by acknowledging his past mistakes and would ask his people to do the same. After which, Jeff would encourage everyone to let go of past issues and forgive themselves and each other. Jeff knew that for Glassco to be at the top of its game, he and his people would need to clean their emotional hulls in their preparation for the race to the top.

Jeff was ready to support them through this phase, no matter what their choices might be. This was going to be a powerful experience for everyone—to have a choice in their direction, and then to decide if they wanted to accept the responsibilities and opportunities of this new direction. This was different from the approach based on "it's my way or the highway."

Jeff realized the Canoe Theory was different from any other business philosophy he had entertained, and that he would need to be open to hearing his people. He realized he was prepared to listen to his people in creating this new direction. He was committed to lead, with their input on the strengths, weakness, opportunities, and threats at Glassco. This experience of being heard by the top executive does not happen very often in business. So the distinction of choice was significant. Everyone was going to be asked, in a non-threatening way, to choose if they wanted to be in the canoe.

Jeff would meet with his senior leaders and discuss their people, who they felt might choose out and who they felt were already on board. Jeff knew these one on one meetings with his people were critical and he and his management team should be prepared and discuss all possibilities. For instance, Jeff had a feeling Carol was on board and excited, but was she challenged and did she feel respected and acknowledged?

Jeff knew he always counted on Carol, but didn't always tell her how important she was to the organization. Jeff felt he might have let her down as her leader. Also there was Jim. Jim was an altogether situation. Jim was good, very good, but didn't seem at all interested or spirited, frankly he seemed burnt out. He had been there even longer than Jeff, but that wasn't the reason, Jeff didn't know why Jim was disinterested and seemly disconnected. Jeff could feel this was going to be a tough conversation, because Jeff didn't want to loose Jim. Jim was amazing with his clients, but Jeff needed Jim to be a positive force when he was in the office.

Jeff spoke with Jim's manager and they reviewed multiple scenarios of Jim's potential reactions. If Jim choose in, what expectations would he need to meet? What new behaviors would he need to exhibit? How could Glassco keep Jim and get Jim interested in being there?

By the end of the day, Jeff and his management team went through the entire list of staff and one by one they discussed what they thought the outcome of each meeting would be and how they could make certain they would do everything in their power to keep everyone without compromising their standards. They all knew the standards and expectations needed to be the same for everyone that was how they could build Glassco to the greatest operation in the industry. Jeff was inspired by the thought of the growth and potential for Glassco, and for every individual that chose to be in the canoe.

As the leader, Jeff now had the basic components of a successful organization stated in a simple, understandable set of tenets—The Canoe Theory.

The challenge ahead was to implement these leadership principles into the culture of Glassco. It was a formidable challenge, but Jeff was confident the results would be worthwhile.

POSTSCRIPT

"Jeff's dream became a reality, and Glassco became one of the few wholly employee-owned ESOPs in the United States. His dream was realized because of the guiding principles of The Canoe Theory."

There are two ways of spreading light: to be the candle or the mirror that reflects it.

Edith Wharton
American Novelist (1862–1937)
Vesalius in Zante

PART
three

The Canoe Theory:
A Practical Application

the
blue print
became reality

" Few things are impossible
to diligence and skill.
Great works are performed
not by strength, but

perseverance. "

Samuel Johnson
English Author (1709–1784)
Most frequently quoted author in English after Shakespeare

the Canoe Theory was created as a vehicle to pull groups of people together toward a common goal. Here are two key examples:

In example one, at a holiday party a fellow named Kevin was sharing his personal experience with his friend about the Canoe Theory. Apparently he had read the Canoe Theory and after doing so said, "My brothers need to read this." He explained that his two brothers owned a business together and that for years they could not get along. As a result, there was tremendous stress in their relationship and in their company.

There were frequent discussions and battles related to who was in command, the direction of their business, levels of authority, and so forth. Kevin gave his brothers a copy of the Canoe Theory to read. "After reading it," Kevin said, "they had a common language and direction."

From Kevin's point of view, each of his brothers took a step back and thought about the principles of the Canoe Theory and what it would take to be in the canoe as a partnership. You could say that they had each made a conscious decision to work together in a more cohesive way. Kevin explained that the Canoe Theory had provided his brothers with a team philosophy formula that connected them. Kevin stated that today his brothers' organization is at last running smoothly in high-production mode, with much less stress.

Example two is a contract furniture company on the East Coast that was on the brink of financial disaster. The company was a small group of individuals who were personally very close and working extremely hard to stay in business. At the time, the market was very difficult for their industry, and several competitors were going out of business.

The partners of this company were stuck, uncertain about what to do to shift their results, so they brought in Dialexis, inc. to consult. With only seventeen employees remaining after layoffs and consolidation of job responsibilities, it was crunch time. Because of the pressures of trying to stay in business, these employees were no longer able to understand and support each other; the staff thought the owners were not committed to their success, and the owners believed the remaining staff did not realize the seriousness of the situation.

After confidentially interviewing all seventeen people (staff and owners), it was apparent they needed to implement the 7 tenets of the Canoe Theory. But first everyone needed to understand why they were not connected as a team and take to heart the severity of the situations the company was in; it was literally fighting for survival.

Once the Canoe Theory was introduced to the entire staff, the owners listened to their people in a way they had not before, with a new appreciation for the feelings of the staff and a new awareness of the business, they were ready to begin building. The partners began to clean up the emotional disconnection; they committed to each other to build, grow, and win as a team. the Canoe Theory was the foundation for this growth. The company survived and, in fact, later merged with another firm in the area. The company is now ranked number one in all categories by which contract furniture companies are measured. Financially, the company's revenues went from a loss to well over one hundred million dollars in business (still during a difficult market), and as a result, today they are the largest operation within their entire competitive field.

After years of consulting with companies, it has become clear that when the Canoe Theory is introduced into organizations, clear structure and a foundational path are provided both for leaders/managers and for staff.

The research completed throughout the United States with numerous organizations suggests that the greatest achievement occurs when a group of individuals work together toward a common goal, with mutual respect and a set of consistent standards. the Canoe Theory provides this set of standards.

TENET 1:
THINK OF
YOUR COMPANY
AS A LONG CANOE

This initial theme is about designing the culture of the canoe—what is the canoe going to look like. How is it going to function? What are acceptable and unacceptable attitudes and behaviors? What behaviors are needed to create the ultimate success? What attitudes are required to draw top talent and new clients to this canoe? This segment of the Canoe Theory philosophy is as critical as all the other tenets combined. This is at the essence of the canoe's core. This is what is commonly defined as the culture of the canoe. Webster's Dictionary suggests that "culture is the predominating attitudes and behaviors that characterize the functioning of a group organization."

All companies have a culture, but the culture is often not developed or well thought out; it typically just happens. But when a culture is designed, meaning that it is created with purpose, with an incredible amount of thought, it will be clear what type of person fits best in culture of the canoe, what type of clients would be attracted to this culture, what style of behavior will thrive, and so on. In order to create and build a specific culture, there are many things to consider, since the canoe's culture is created by attitudes and behaviors, core values, beliefs, and the established rules of conduct.

The great opportunity is creating a culture that supports your beliefs, as a leader or as the existing core team of a canoe. All companies have cultures. Think back on a pleasant experience you had recently involving a company. What type of culture did that company, restaurant, movie theatre or daycare center have? The interesting part of selecting where we work or shop, or the kinds of people we hire, is that it works best if there is a commonality or shared appreciation of core beliefs which helps to define the culture. In other words, we tend to relate to people or companies that share our common values and attitudes, and we appreciate their style of interaction if it is similar to our own. That does not mean there are not differences, but if the core values, beliefs, attitudes, and behaviors are similar, there will likely be a stronger connection and appreciation.

There are many cultural differences that distinguish organizations and competitors from one another. Suffice to say, there are tremendous cultural diversities and challenges among all canoes. (However, as we noted in our introduction for Spanish readers, we firmly believe the concepts of the Canoe Theory are universally applicable.) And the Canoe Theory supports honing the culture of a company and reminding everyone that selecting a culture that fits with their beliefs helps everyone realize they can make a choice. Culture should be at the core of making a good selection.

When an individual or management team begins building, rebuilding, or refining in order to become a more effective organization, a true perspective on how the culture is perceived is needed. Recall Jeff from Glassco: even though he was an accomplished leader who knew his company well, he still had the wisdom to seek and collect his employees' perceptions. All canoes are uniquely structured; expectations differ, styles differ, and therefore cultures differ.

A defined corporate culture is extremely important to the success of the canoe. It establishes the system of interactions within the canoe—and is made up of attitudes and behaviors.

This system of interaction should be based on the canoe's rules of conduct. It is the foundation of what is and what is not acceptable.

Three key areas to fostering a successful culture:

- People
- Environment
- Customers

Sometimes we become oblivious to our environment or our philosophy of how we treat people or customers within our canoe. We walk right on top of coffee-stained carpets or by cluttered storage rooms. We ignore the image of our office and the message it sends. Employees should be aware that a genuine quest for quality should take place at all levels, and on all fronts of an organization.

Often we forget to review corporate expectations such as the friendliness with which we answer the phones, or how we respond to our customers. Or worse yet, we accept rudeness or curt interactions with our teammates, or we allow "power down" leadership—the kind of overaggressive, domineering management that makes people feel small and useless. These are all very important signals as to what is really valued by an organization, and are therefore at the core of its culture. To ignore these key signals can be the beginning of the end.

Our future is predicated on being aware of our present culture and determining if this culture is going to take us where we want to go. When John Scully was CEO of Apple, he was known to say "the greatness is in the details." It's the details, the little things that make up the big things. Little things create our environment, little things create the attitudes we allow and the behaviors we accept. They all come together to make up or create our culture. The significance of our culture is huge.

Our culture attracts our new hires and clients. This should inspire some of you to ask questions such as these: Is our culture positioning us to attract the best of the best? Did our last new hires have the qualities we wanted or did we just settle?

Let us start at the beginning. Let's begin with a review of what we have; what is our existing culture, talent pool, attitudes and behaviors? Then we have a good shot to rebuild or redefine what it is we want our canoe to look like?

THOUGHTS FOR LEADERS

- Stand back and take a fresh look at your existing culture starting with the environment of your canoe.

- Take a Sunday Walk-Through in your office. On any non-business day, walk through your facility and look around. Ask yourself, "What is the environment communicating?"
  Evaluate with the eyes of someone from outside your operation or department. Bring a collegue in to share what they see—it could be an eye-opening experience for both of you.

- Be objective as you look around, as if you had no connection to the organization or department. Take in what you experience. Become more aware and astute. This is your first impression, and a valuable one. Your environment is always representing you, including how your organization handles after-hours interactions, what your voice-activated answering service communicates, and how you provide early-morning deliveries to clients needing support outside business hours.

Important questions to ask:

- Is the entrance or lobby inviting?

- Is there a locked entrance during business hours?

- Is the reception area welcoming or intimidating?

- Is the reception desk or entrance organized and clean?

- Are there dead plants in the corners?

- How does the layout of each department affect communication?

- Does the business environment represent a culture you are proud of?

- Is this the way you intended to have your organization represented?

Review the image you are presenting to the public. These next set of questions are at the foundation of what the canoe represents.

The next questions are people- and customer-focused:

- Is there someone assigned to greet everyone entering the lobby or place of business in a friendly manner?

- Is your receptionist a people-person or a guard dog?

- If visitors entering the reception area are required to wait, are they offered refreshments? Is there space to wait?

- How does it feel when you call into your office? Is the initial reception warm and inviting, supportive, helpful, and customer-focused? If not, why is this?

- If you overhear an internal conversation among employees, is it respectful and cooperative, or is it demeaning, judgmental, and critical?

- Is the experience of doing business with your company easy and enjoyable, or difficult and stressful?

- Is the organization client-centered?

- Is the organization focused on employee development and retention?

- Does the organization meet your original expectations?

- Ask yourself, would I want to do business with a company with these qualities?

Next, consider taking the customer challenge:

- Have an executive from your firm take the time to have a conversation with some of your key customers and get their perspectives on your organization.

- Ask new employees what their perception of the company was before being hired, and then after being hired. (If you've created an environment of honesty and trust, you will get great information. If that isn't the case, this will be ineffective.)

- Ask a potential candidate who didn't take the job offered why not, and what his or her perception of your organization was.

- Ask vendors how they would rank your organization on competency, attitude, and ease of doing business.

- Hire an outside group to get feedback from existing clients or potential new clients.

- If you are in a professional group, ask a colleague to "shop" your organization—the shopper might act as a prospective client calling for pricing, asking for a proposal, or applying for an open position within the company. Ask for input on his or her perception of the existing culture.

The ultimate objective is to test your perception against those of your employees as well as against those of your clients or customers to get an authentic reading of your starting point—this is the present state of your canoe. Remember, as a leader, it is critical to hear the honest feedback of employees and customers. They often are the key to unlocking your greatness.

THOUGHTS FOR ASSOCIATES

The culture truly defines the essence of the organization—the canoe and what are acceptable and expected behaviors and attitudes. By joining or being in the canoe, you are essentially saying, "I am buying into the canoe's beliefs." Here's an idea of what you can do (even if you are already an employee):

•   Confirm that your values and beliefs are in line with those of the canoe. If you don't believe or have similar values as the canoe, it will be difficult for you to support the canoe or be successful in the canoe.

•   Talk to your leader if there are differences and discuss those differences; by doing so, you will be able to gain clarity on the differences. (This might be an excellent opportunity for you to support the canoe by sharing your beliefs, thoughts, and ideas.) However, if there is too much of a gap between your beliefs and values and the canoe's beliefs, values, and culture, you might be best served to reconsider being part of this canoe.

•   Take a chance to make a difference. Stand up for something you believe in and share it with your supervisor or with a supervisor you trust.

•   Ask for coaching from Human Resources or someone senior that you admire. Ask for confidentiality and for feedback on how you might present your ideas or thoughts on the environment or culture of your canoe. (This is a bold move, but this is how you can begin building your reputation as someone that can lead, listen, and contribute. This is the stuff leaders are made of. This step of courage could be the first step toward being considered for a promotion or being seen as a potential candidate for a leadership position. But at the same time, be judicious. Look for concrete evidence that your perceptions are grounded in reality before choosing to share them with others.)

- Determine if the canoe's style represents a culture where you can personally succeed. For a team to be successful, it needs individuals that are suited and committed. This is the time to determine if this is your canoe, and if you are ready to make a solid contribution to the canoe.

- Know that you have a choice, and it's up to you to use your head in selecting your canoe. It's a very significant decision.

- Take the time to make the right choice.

- Evaluate if this is a platform where your skill set fits. It's up to you to ask yourself the most important question: "Do I fit?"

THE BOTTOM LINE

Establishing the culture is a key component of the Canoe Theory. The culture needs to be designed by the leader of the canoe. Gathering feedback, thoughts, and ideas from all associates is an important step in the design and creation of the canoe's culture, but it is the leader who has the final say about what that culture is going to be. Therein lies the difference among canoes. Thus, it is essential that as an associate you know what kind of canoe you are joining, or, if you are the leader, what kind of canoe you are creating. The culture of the canoe is the foundation for everything, including hiring talent, attracting clients, and creating the style and acceptable practice of employee interaction. It is much like the Ten Commandments serving as the basis of Mosaic law. The culture establishes the rules of play.

Do your best to understand the overall objective of the canoe, its style and identity—in all, its culture.

As you discover the environment/culture that exists—whether you are manager or associate—ask yourself if it supports your values, your beliefs, and your purpose/passion.

Being in a canoe where there are mutually respected goals, values, and beliefs will make challenging times much easier for both you and your fellow paddlers.

It is important to understand that among all functional canoes, common denominators do exist. As a leader, it is your responsibility to provide the items below. As an associate, you have the right to experience this type of leadership.

•   Functional canoes rely on strong, fair leadership with a strong culture and a clear vision.

•   Functional canoes have a platform of respect and teamwork.

Remember, no company or position you might hold is perfect, and no canoe or position will ever be flawless. Being challenged and occasionally finding yourself uncomfortable is not the same as being in a canoe that doesn't share your values or suggests that you don't fit in your position. Challenges are a healthy and often important component of a canoe, and being uncomfortable with challenges or change often indicates you are growing. And that is healthy. But take note if these challenges persist beyond what seems reasonable, or if you find yourself without a positive rationale as to why you are uncomfortable. Passing challenges are healthy, whereas lingering challenges may injure both you and the rest of those in the canoe. A wise paddler learns to differentiate between the two types of obstacles.

One way to clarify a situation when you are struggling is simply to communicate with the appropriate person. The appropriate person can be the person you are having challenges with or your supervisors. A successful, well-functioning canoe has challenges and difficulties, but also has a way to connect through honest, respectful communication in order to help people get past problems or roadblocks. This typically reveals misunderstandings and eliminates frustrations. When you overcome challenges within your organization, you are not only growing as an individual, but you are adding value to the canoe and to yourself.

The limit to which you have accepted being comfortable is the limit to which you have grown.

" The ultimate measure of

a man is not

where he **stands**

in moments of comfort and

convenience, but where

he stands at times of

challenge and controversy. "

Martin Luther King Jr.
Civil Rights Pioneer (1929–1968)
Strength to Love, 1963

TENET 2:
THE CANOE HAS A
DIRECTION, A DESTINATION

A shared vision is one of the most powerful forces an organization can unleash on a daily basis. Ideally, if there is an opportunity for individuals to have a voice in the development of the vision, your organization will have moved from being a mission-statement-driven organization to an organization with a crusade. Without a doubt, crusades will always be more powerful than mission statements, because crusades touch people from a personal perspective.

The organization must establish a vision that captures the emotions of all members. This desired state must be challenging, achievable, and stimulating, so that everyone in the canoe is motivated to reach the destination.

In order for a canoe to move forward and effectively serve its intended purpose, it needs to have a clearly defined destination with power. This is where it is necessary to tap into the talent of the entire organization to connect emotionally to this vision or direction.

Typically, that destination is established by the top of the organization, but in some cases it is up to a division, a department, or for that matter an individual to be the visionary for the collective group.

If, indeed, there is no clear vision of where the canoe (your organization, department, or group) is going, you may be the individual who needs to step up and get involved by taking the lead. Leaders don't always have a title. Some of the most impressive leaders in the world have been regular people with a vision or a crusade that benefited the larger group. A successful canoe requires the coordination of all members of the canoe toward the canoe's direction. Although all paddlers are equally responsible for giving their best efforts to help the canoe arrive at the shared destination, leaders are additionally responsible for communicating, charting, and evaluating the progress and direction of the canoe.

THOUGHTS FOR LEADERS

- Take responsibility for establishing a clear direction for your group. This is a key element in the success of the canoe. Your people look to you for clarity of purpose and direction. Take the time to step back and create a road map of where everyone needs to go.

- Make sure the destination of the canoe is well defined, and that your employees know how to support getting to this destination. This needs to be specific for each position and role. It seems this component might get lost in the translation. The key is *specific for each role*. Guidance and direction with specificity is the small but powerful detail that will ensure results.

- Remember that just because you have the organization's mission statement immortalized in granite in the lobby doesn't mean the employees know where the canoe is going or what their roles are in making it happen. This is easily checked by asking some of the people within your organization their thoughts on what the mission of the organization is.

- Once you have the vision of the canoe in place, talk about it constantly. Make it live within the entire organization. Make it exciting and worth the undertaking.

Let's take a minute to define the word "destination" in a different way. Imagine all the personnel from the company standing at the base of a mountain. The top executive says, "Our goal is to reach the summit. That will be the defining moment when we can say the organization has succeeded."

The leader understands better than anyone that the climb will have moments when it will be extremely difficult. He or she knows there will be periods when things will go smoothly, and there will be stages when everyone will be challenged.

When asked if they are up for the climb, most employees will say, "I'm in!"—especially new employees. The problem is that employees often buy in without fully understanding that what lies ahead may be more challenging than what they signed up for.

On any climb, the difficulty increases as the climber ascends higher.

When times get tough, the climb is extreme and demanding, employees often complain, become negative, stop caring, or even bail out.

What causes these disconnects? What keeps people from maintaining their original commitment to fight to the summit as they initially said they would?

Employees often lose interest because they end up feeling that they are not the ones that are winning. They believe the owner or company is winning, and their attitude becomes "why should I care?" Often they don't feel listened to. They feel the only voice that is heard is the leaders.

This attitude usually takes hold when the going gets tough. The question is, what can leaders do about it?

The best idea is to discover what individuals perceive a winning outcome is for them. If you think money motivates your people, you may be right or wrong—however, it could be more important than that.

When you discover what personally motivates each employee to continue the climb—especially in difficult or challenging times—you will have discovered the turbocharger that will keep them going through times good and bad.

- Care enough to ask employees what they work for—in other words, what's in it for them when the organization reaches the summit.

- Find out what employees want from working and supporting the organization in the deepest sense. Again, it may be financial, family-specific, or social, but you need to learn why people are in the canoe.

- Pay attention to what employees say. When you discover what motivates them, understand what their dreams are, and show them that by helping the canoe reach its destination they will realize their aspirations, they will connect and participate with a revitalized commitment.

- Support employees' dreams. Certainly, employees should support the company vision—after all, that is what they committed to do when they got in the canoe—but they should also be committed to their own dreams or visions.

- Once you have done your best to discover your employees' personal dreams, tell them that you view your role as their leader as having the responsibility to support them in realizing their dreams or visions.

- Do this with as many members of your team as possible, and you will have found the secret to a new level of commitment from those who are making the climb with you.

- Create an environment that fosters honest communication. Oppression stymies creative thinking and new ideas, and in turn cuts off the circulation of a company's lifeblood: creativity.

THOUGHTS FOR ASSOCIATES

- Make a commitment. Being committed to the company's destination is expected. It's your job to support the canoe in reaching its destination—that's what you get paid for.

- Take part in discovering your dreams, vision, or passion (your destination). Once you are committed to your own destination, you will find supporting the canoe in order to reach its destination will be more satisfying.

- Find your dream, vision, or purpose. This can be difficult. Begin with a blank pad of paper and ask yourself "What do I want and when do I want it?" and write it down. It may seem crazy, but you do have the answers. Ask yourself what your special gifts are that you can share and contribute to this opportunity. Take the time to focus on discovering your purpose, your vision, and your dreams. Then begin to be aware of how to best manifest it while supporting the vision of the canoe.

- Follow a plan if you are seeking a new canoe—be it a new division within the company, a new role as leader or associate, or a job change. A thorough investigation of your dream will substantially increase the probability of finding a canoe that represents a good fit—that is, the right canoe for you. Take the responsibility to understand what you want from a canoe. Then go find it or create it from the canoe you are presently in.

You are in a more powerful position than you might think. Canoes are always looking for great people that will support their direction/destination. If you are a committed, talented individual, you can select where to put your efforts. Just make certain the canoe you select supports your personal goals. That is the win-win.

When selecting a canoe, seek answers to these questions:

•	What's the existing culture of this canoe?

•	Where is this canoe going?

•	When and how does it plan to reach its destination?

•	Do the leaders and team members seem like individuals that you want to rely on, work with, and interact with?

•	Does your intuition (gut feeling) say yes?

•	Does the canoe appear sturdy enough to stay afloat in rough waters or adverse conditions?

•	In your conversations, do your best to determine if the leaders understand where the canoe is going and establish whether they seem to have a clear view of how they will support the canoe. Ideally, the canoe's destination will include the realization of each member's personal objectives. By supporting the canoe's destination, you should be able to reach your personal and professional goals as well.

•	Take the time to understand what you want to achieve within this canoe. Make this a priority. Since you are expected to pay the price, you'll need to discover what you want personally and when you want it.

- Ask yourself if the price you will be required to pay in this canoe will contribute to your personal dream (your destination).

- Remember that the organization has a right to expect your total commitment. So be certain you can give your total commitment. And make certain your personal dreams can be realized as well.

When you get to the top of the summit, there should be two flags in the ground: one for the company and one for you. Yes, one for you, too. The responsibility of making sure you have your flag at the top of the mountain is yours. If you believe your leaders do not support your personal flag, be open to the possibility that they haven't read the Canoe Theory, and they need help; consider supporting their growth. If you can support your manager to be more successful, he or she should be in a great place to support you with your dreams. In other words, be proactive. This is your opportunity to contribute to your success and the success of your canoe.

THE BOTTOM LINE

All canoes should have a clear and defined destination. If yours doesn't, make it happen, whether you're an associate or leader.

The destination is best accomplished if every member of the canoe is able to connect a personal win to the achievement of the canoe's destination.

Segments of this journey may not always be smooth.

Know that it's up to you to find the canoe that fits you. Also know that if you don't fit in your current canoe, it's up to you to find a solution, or the canoe may pull over and let you out.

Clear and constant communication is critical to the success of the journey and must be a top priority. Reminder, it's everyone's responsibility to communicate or create an atmosphere for communication and dialogue.

Despite posting the destination (the crusade), just talking about it or meeting about it doesn't mean everyone gets it or understands their part in contributing to the crusade.

Often individuals join a firm with vigor at the start, only to lose faith during the tough parts of the climb. A sustained effort requires a personal connection with the destination of the canoe and a realization that it all comes together when we all come together.

Everyone can win when they all join together. It's an attitude of win-win vs. win-lose.

TENET 3:

EVERYONE HAS A SEAT AND A PADDLE,

AND EVERYONE

IS EXPECTED TO PADDLE

It is impossible for the canoe to reach its destination if everyone does not fulfill the expectations associated with participation. the Canoe Theory establishes that everyone is directly involved in the success of the organization. This is the underlying foundation of the philosophy. As obvious as it may seem, most companies do not rely on everyone or on the entire team. There is an undercurrent in a majority of companies that depends on a few to be responsible and the rest just follow along. The premise that everyone is directly involved is typically a shift in thinking for most individuals and companies.

A necessary understanding is that we're all in the same canoe, and thus responsible and accountable for our own and each other's performance. We are inextricably dependent upon one another for success, and we cannot reach our potential if, collectively, we are not all in the canoe.

Roles and responsibilities reflect seats and paddles, and each individual must understand how the execution of his or her duties moves the canoe forward.

Simply put, no one rides for minimal or no effort. You cannot sit on the side and dangle your feet.

Everyone must continuously perform to the limits of their capabilities or the leaders must immediately investigate why there is an issue. Is this a performance issue, a training issue, or a personal crisis issue? This is key to supporting the canoe and the paddler/associate. Best said, the canoe cannot operate at full capacity with poor performers, because it is not fair to the associates who are contributing completely, and it is not a method by which everyone can win.

To reach its destination with the greatest possible efficiency, the canoe must allocate and use its resources effectively. To do this, all members must contribute to the canoe's progress.

Each member must have a clear understanding of where he or she fits within the canoe, and how he or she is expected to paddle.

It is equally important that members understand how their contribution supports other teammates within the canoe, and ultimately how their function/role affects the overall progress of the canoe.

Functions and roles vary. No matter what the function or role is, every member has one. There can be no passive weight inside a well-functioning canoe. Whether it is a leader providing the canoe's direction or an employee providing inspiration, everyone can and does make a difference. The question is what kind of difference does everyone make? Is it positive and productive or negative and destructive?

Each individual must support the efficient allocation of the canoe's finite resources; members must sit where they fit or are needed at the time.

The seat where an individual is best able to serve the canoe may not be the person's first choice. However, an individual's skill must be used in the most effective manner to support the canoe in reaching its destination.

Each seat and paddle serves an important purpose. There are no special seats and no special paddles. This means that every contributing member of the canoe should be considered as important as any other. There are no exceptions.

THOUGHTS FOR LEADERS

- Establish the canoe's rights and responsibilities. These are the guiding principles for behavior and the expectations for each participant in the canoe, including leaders. By noting that each member of the canoe has both the right to and responsibility for the same notions, you will emphasize each person's role in maintaining the kind of canoe in which he or she wants to thrive. Examples of what the rights and responsibilities of the canoe might be are:

You have the right to honest communication.

You have the responsibility to provide honest communication.

- Create a short list of practical, effective guidelines for con- duct. Create a maximum of ten rights and responsibilities for the canoe. These should support the culture of the canoe. The rights and responsibilities are best designed around what behaviors are necessary to complete our journey.

For example, a technically brilliant group was having a challenge with communication and trust. The rights and responsibilities they created focused on the issues they felt they needed support with:

You have the right to expect honesty from others, and
You have the responsibility to be honest with others.

You have the right to expect integrity, and
You have the responsibility to demonstrate integrity.

You have the right to be heard and understood, and
You have the responsibility to listen effectively to others.

You have the right to a positive environment, and,
You have the responsibility to communicate and behave in a positive manner.

You have the right to receive honest, open communication, and
You have the responsibility to provide and be open to honest communication.

These were designed to support this particular team in breaking out of some of the behaviors that would not serve them as a productive team. In this case, there were fifteen team members, and each member contributed to creating these rights and responsibilities. In a larger organization, you can ask each group to contribute one or two areas to be considered for the rights and responsibilities, but then the complete list ultimately should be created by the management team and rolled out to everyone at a general meeting. Rights and responsibilities are very powerful, and the one area that needs to be discussed is that everyone must abide by all the rights and responsibilities, especially management. No one is exempt from the rights and responsibilities once they are rolled out if they are to be respected.

- Establish the consequences for violating any of the rights and responsibilities. If individuals do not work within those guidelines, then what's the consequence? (Remember, even your most revered individuals are held to these standards.)

- Identify each member's talent and place each person in the canoe where his or her talents are maximized. This is usually very fruitful for the canoe and for the individual. Everyone loves to win, be successful, or look good in front of their peers.

- Form a team of individuals that will do whatever it takes to support the canoe. This is accomplished by outlining what is expected and making known the consequences for not performing. Remember, attitude is just as critical as work performance (paddling).

- Help employees understand that it doesn't matter where team members sit in the canoe. If employees are vested in the company, they will exhibit an attitude of "what can I do to help?" rather than "it's not my job."

- Determine what might be causing nonproductive attitudes or behaviors. One of the main reasons an employee becomes negative or destructive may be because he or she doesn't feel vested in the direction/destination of the canoe. It's up to you as a leader to determine what the issues are that are causing a member of your team to be destructive.

- Handle complainers immediately. (These are separate from employees who may express legitimate concerns.) They can be a drain on the team, and the team expects you as the leader to get their teammate to snap out of it, get on board, and drop the petty whining. When an individual is complaining about where he or she sits or what's wrong with the paddle, you need to get to the bottom of the real issue and handle it.

  As a leader, it's a priority to get everyone in line and paddling. If there are an excess of complainers you might want to design rights and responsibilities to address this condition.

- Avoid operating with the formula L + AWAE = E
  (Loyalty + A Well-Articulated Excuse = Employability).

- Consider using this formula instead: A + P = E
  (*Attitude + Performance = Employability*).

- Build a high-performing team. A team of high-performing individuals works with what they are given—they make it work.

Your success as a leader is based on handling issues immediately, being fair, and making the difficult decisions. However, if the organization simply does not have the resources to provide the ideal tools or situation at that moment, you'll need to explain the situation to your team.

- Inform them that the tools they have are the best the organization can offer them at this given time. Look at this as an opportunity to be creative.

- Remind them of the direction/destination of the canoe and why it's important.

- Communicate to them that if we all pay the price in various ways, we all will win as a team and individually. You can do this by explaining the sacrifices others have made or by drawing on examples in which a previous sacrifice resulted in an ultimate gain. Remember, if they have created their own flags (what they are personally doing this for), they will be more inclined to pay the price and potentially come up with some creative solutions to get past the blocks.

- If they continue to complain, try to help them understand the real issue that is bothering them, or, as a last resort, you may need to consider the alternative of release. Let them get into a canoe they like; allow them to choose to step out of your canoe.

- Always consider your Human Resources policies and procedures. Make certain all conversations are documented and check legal resources. You need to know prior to any serious conversations with your employees what your options are. In other words, what are your rights, the rights of your associates, the policies of your organization, and the limits you have as a leader. Preparation is essential when you are challenged by a disgruntled employee. One thing is certain: it is your responsibility as a leader to do what is right for the canoe and the employee. And remember to always remain calm and professional.

THOUGHTS FOR ASSOCIATES

- Expect to paddle. As members of the canoe, all team members are expected to paddle, no matter what. If, for some reason, you don't paddle or won't paddle, you will be asked to leave the canoe.

- Remember that when you join the canoe, you make a commitment to act in accordance to the rules (rights and responsibilities) of the canoe. One key rule of all canoes is that you have to paddle.

- Continue to paddle even if you discover you have made a mistake in joining the canoe. You are still required to paddle until you find a different canoe.

- Realize that organizations don't always have the perfect tools that employees desire. Sometimes the seat and paddle won't be optimum. There may be poor or no marketing materials, outdated equipment, or a general lack of resources for you to do your job. You might be challenged to deal with those types of issues for some time. One suggestion is to communicate to your supervisor or leader, to share this information with him or her, and explain how not having access to specific tools makes it difficult for you to contribute in a bigger way. Ask if and when the situation might change. Communication is a very important part of understanding. This might be a great place to step back emotionally and look at the canoe in its complete form. Typically companies don't withhold resources from their people, but there are often times when resources (money) are limited, and when you are not looking at the entire company, it might seem as though your needs are not being considered.

- If you are having a difficult time in the canoe and, as a result, are unwilling to paddle, examine why. The odds are it may be more about you than about the canoe. Look at your contribution to any issues before you make decisions that the canoe is in error.

- Take the opportunity to be 100 percent responsible. Your job is paddling. What do you need to do to be successful? Maybe learn more about your product or job function? Gain technical skills? Improve your work ethic? What is standing in the way of your being a successful contributor? Take a look at why you wouldn't want to paddle and give it your all. Your actions today are creating your reputation for tomorrow. Maybe you want to ask yourself, what is it I want my reputation to be?

- Speak up and discuss what you need to be successful with your supervisor if you are not given the proper guidance or opportunities. If your supervisor is the issue, take the risk and ask Human Resources or another supervisor for coaching on how to approach this issue. Take the opportunity to speak up for your own growth and development. For this to be successful, first get all your facts on paper. Then approach Human Resources or a respected leader and request a time to meet. If the leader asks why, tell him or her in a fairly casual way that you want feedback. Do not begin the conversation at that time. When you do meet with the leader, tell him or her that you need coaching on a personal matter, and you would like this conversation to be confidential. Once you get his or her word it will be confidential, begin with your problem. A note about good leaders: they will support each other and they won't take sides, so if you're looking for someone to side with you or tell you that you are right about your supervisor being a jerk, it won't happen. Your goal should be to gain good, solid council on how to approach your supervisor. Unfortunately, supervisors don't always have the skills to be great leaders. It is a challenge, but if you are capable of working through an issue like this, your growth will be tremendous. This experience is truly one of "managing up."

• Respond to challenges. In any canoe, there is always an opportunity to shine and to show your stuff—what you're made of and how well you can perform. It is truly up to you. A note about shining. When you step up and do amazing problem solving or complete a difficult project, don't forget to acknowledge your teammates—usually you will have had help in this achievement.

• Deal effectively with issues. If you are angry, resentful, or have grievances about the canoe, team members, or your supervisor, take the time to come to terms with the situation and emotionally let it go. This is a difficult process. But, your choice is to stay angry and perhaps be right about someone being a knucklehead, or work through it and let it go. It takes a lot of energy to be angry at someone or something for a long period of time. And you will not be able to be your best if you are saddled with negative thoughts or grudges. It wastes your energy and focuses on the past, not on the present or the future. Taking the opportunity to let it go is essential for you to be successful and get what you want.

Here's one strategy for letting go:

- Discuss the situation with someone who will be honest with you (not just take your side) and will give you good feedback.

- Write your thoughts down on paper and let them settle overnight. The next day, read what you've written and determine whether it is really as bad as you thought.

- Last, consider forgiving the person or issue so you can get on with your life. Negative thoughts or issues drain you of your potential because you are just stuck there. This is self-limiting and will not serve you. The choice is yours.

THE BOTTOM LINE

As a leader, you are expected to ensure that all the team members paddle. If someone isn't paddling, the others look to you to make it happen or to move the person out of the canoe. If you have favorites, you will be certain not to have everyone's support. Even children know that when the rules aren't fair, they won't want to play.

Leaders need to understand what motivates the individuals on their team and place them accordingly within the canoe.

In order to establish a baseline of knowledge about each member's position, a leader can support the canoe by cross-training the team in critical areas. By doing this, leaders are able to create a more functional and efficient team. Cross-training also helps identify and develop the breadth of talent of each team member.

Leaders must be honest about their capabilities and about those of their employees. If someone is a good paddler but doesn't fit into their current seat, you are responsible for moving that person to the most productive seat available. And if a person has legitimate directional concerns, you are obligated to listen and act accordingly.

Employees must be honest with themselves and their teammates.

If an employee knows that he or she does not fit in the canoe, the employee needs to find a canoe to belong in. If an employee doesn't like his or her situation, it is incumbent upon the employee to seek the desired change. If it is not granted, the person has a choice: go back to work and maintain a positive attitude or look for another canoe that is more suitable for them.

This may seem harsh, but the reality is there may be a cultural fit. Destination and direction are sometimes created solely by top management who haven't realized the value of listening to their people. Therefore, it's up to all employees to be true to themselves first, because only then they can be great team members. If you can't support the canoe, being in that canoe will not support you.

" The **greatness** is in the details. **"**

TENET 4:

THOSE WHO WON'T PADDLE HAVE TO GET OUT OF THE CANOE

To arrive at their shared destination, everyone is required to paddle on a continual basis. There is not sufficient room in the canoe for an individual to just sit and not paddle. This notion underscores the importance of a positive attitude and a commitment to action.

An effective canoe supports the weight of all members as it moves toward its overall destination, but, remember, no passive weight is allowed. Given this, those who will not or cannot paddle must get out of the canoe.

A functional canoe will not support the negative effects any member might generate. Those who will not paddle drain the potential and morale of the whole and, in the end, destroy their own potential as well.

In a dysfunctional canoe, those who won't paddle can hide—sometimes for years. Members of functional canoes discover the nonpaddlers quickly and their leaders take action.

THOUGHTS FOR LEADERS

- Evaluate who is in the canoe; listen and look for signals of low production and bad attitudes.

- Make decisions relative to the employee on the basis of A + P = E (*Attitude + Performance = Employability*).

- Remove a member of the canoe who will not paddle. Taking this action serves the whole and—more importantly—supports the individual who will not paddle it allows them the opportunity to get into a canoe where they can be happy. Ask the non-paddler to resign or re-engage. As a leader, it is your responsibility to ensure that everyone is paddling. If a non-paddler will not resign or re-engage, document the lack of performance and work with Human Resources to move that person out of the canoe as quickly as possible.

- Train your managers on how to identify non-paddlers. These may include behaviors such as being unwilling to solve problems for themselves, sitting idle while important responsibilities wait, and allowing shared responsibilities to pile up on others. Understand that taking action regarding non-paddlers will yield a resurgence of respect for management.

- Listen to your people. Employees know who's in the canoe, who's doing his or her best to contribute, and who's just giving lip service.

- Protect the stability of the canoe and make the tough decisions so that the organization and the team prosper.

- Support other employees by having the courage to terminate unproductive individuals. (Always seek legal advice and train your managers on proper conduct when dealing with employee performance measurement and termination protocols.)

THOUGHTS FOR ASSOCIATES

- Take responsibility for understanding what constitutes the standards of acceptable paddling (performance and attitude).

- Do whatever is necessary within legal, moral, and ethical boundaries to achieve the benchmarks management has provided.

- Realize that the higher your position in the organization, the more you become an extension of leadership. This means that if you are a senior paddler, you are looked at as an extension of management. Being on time for meetings and contributing beyond your job scope demonstrate the attitudes and behaviors expected of everyone who wants to be part of the canoe.

- Take responsibility for challenging leadership when things are not going well (for example, if someone is not paddling). Most of the time, the leaders are not as aware of difficulties in the trenches as you are. If you speak up and there are no changes, you need to make a choice to continue being in the canoe or remove yourself (keeping in mind the proper timing for your best interests).

- Be an effective team member. As a team member, you will be expected to support leadership, attend meetings, be positive, and contribute to the canoe as a professional, despite the fact that you may be a top performer.

- Be careful of the messages you are sending without saying a word. Participating in gossip or negative talk within the ranks is unacceptable. Even listening passively to gossip or negative talk is a form of acceptance and agreement.

- Recognize your role to support the canoe. Despite any perceived leadership issues you may have, as long as you are a part of the canoe you have an obligation to appropriately support the canoe, be it by engaging leadership on important issues or paddling with your best efforts. As a point of clarity, challenging leadership needs to be done professionally and with specific issues in mind, not just by whining. Once you've made your case to your leader, you have the choice to accept their decision and support it—even if the outcome is not what you wanted—

or make a choice that this is not your type of canoe and professionally choose to get out of the canoe.

THE BOTTOM LINE

No passive or dead weight is allowed in the canoe. Everyone in the canoe must serve a purpose and support the canoe in its endeavor. The canoe cannot be all that it can be without everyone's contribution.

The standards that will define acceptable and unacceptable behavior should be set in place by the leaders, and these should be completely understood by all team members.

Realize that no single individual wants to sit in a canoe and look across at another paddler and say to himself or herself, "Why is this person in this canoe?" Competent employees expect competency around them.

Each member of your team wants to be surrounded by people who inspire, motivate, contribute, energize others, act as team players who are kind and ethical, and who pull their own weight. This makes being in the canoe more fun.

Paddling can be defined as reaching the benchmarks that are set. If you don't or won't attempt to reach the benchmarks, you should expect to be removed from the canoe. That includes everyone, leaders and team members alike.

The canoe will not reach its destination with mediocre, substandard performance. Leaders need to make certain everyone knows how to be successful and give everyone the best tools, training, and direction on what it takes to be the best. Leaders need to have that conversation with everyone to ensure all team members are clear about what it takes to be successful in their seats and with their paddles. If your leader doesn't have that conversation with you, ask for clarification about the expectations for your role so you have no reason not to be successful.

TENET 5:
THOSE WHO PADDLE WELL BUT
PREVENT OTHERS FROM PADDLING
HAVE TO ADJUST OR GET OUT OF THE CANOE

Reaching a destination depends upon everyone's coordinated efforts. When paddlers are synchronized and coordinated, the canoe moves smoothly and surely toward its destination. Synergy is achieved when people act in unison as a team to achieve a shared vision. Those who are not team players—who do not paddle in unison, don't follow the canoe's paddling rules, or just do it their way—must adjust or get out of the canoe.

The most dangerous individual in the canoe is one who is negative or interferes with the positive performance of other team members. If this individual will not adjust, he or she must be removed from the canoe. Once again, A + P = E *(Attitude + Performance = Employment)*.

No one should be exempt from the standards established for the canoe, no matter what their revenue performance, family connection, or position. This is not the easiest challenge for a leader but, if handled properly, can be the most powerful action a leader can take to benefit the entire organization. Everyone expects a leader to make certain there is fairness in expectations, which is why the rights and responsibilities are so critical to a well-functioning canoe. These are the guidelines that all members have to follow. The respect garnered by living by the rights and responsibilities is profound and will support the achievement of the canoe's goals. If the top leader is the problem, then the canoe has a big problem. The leader creates the culture, and if the leader is abusive, the culture will most likely tolerate abuse, disrespect, or unprofessional behavior. If the canoe is led by this type of leader, the Canoe Theory won't work. the Canoe Theory principles are built on teamwork, supporting the whole, and respecting every member.

Years ago, there was a leader (let's call him Arthur) who asked, "How do I control my partner (let's call him Sam)? He is abusive, rude, and impatient with everyone, except me." The problem was that since the company was financially successful, there was really no motivation for Sam to adjust his style. Arthur realized how unjust Sam was to his employees, but did not want to challenge or confront Sam. Arthur ultimately hired an outside consulting group to come in, hoping this would solve the problem, Sam would adjust his unprofessional style of interacting with people, and everyone would live happily ever after. After multiple candid meetings with the consultants and Arthur, Sam realized how destructive his behavior had been and how difficult it was for everyone, including Arthur, to work in such a destructive environment. However, Sam didn't really want to change, and after some time Arthur realized he no longer could support his partner.

Then he remembered the Canoe Theory Tenet #3: "Everyone has a seat and a paddle, and everyone is expected to paddle." Arthur knew he could no longer support Sam's behavior because the culture caused by that behavior was not in alignment with his beliefs. Arthur resigned and sold his share of the business. Arthur believed in the Canoe Theory and did not want to be part of a canoe that did not respect people. Today, Arthur is the president of a vibrant, thriving, functional business and stands up for the professional treatment of his teammates.

If you are an employee and have a dysfunctional leader, you can certainly have a conversation with Human Resources. If you decide to meet with your direct report Instead (your boss) here are a few suggestions to consider before your meeting:

1. What is the outcome you want?
2. What will you do if you don't get what you want?
3. Be honest and authentic with your feedback.
4. Own your feelings, speak directly, and don't blame "I feel frustrated when I'm not copied on important e-mails."
5. Speak only for you—not, "we feel."
6. Make recommendations as to how you feel the issues can be resolved.
7. Share what you do see as positive points.
8. Thank your boss for the meeting.

Finally, if you are an employee and just cannot take the emotional drain of working in this type of environment, your choice is to look for another seat and paddle or, ultimately, for another canoe.

You might be surprised how many leaders do not realize the damage they are creating or the craziness they are allowing. Consider having a candid, professional conversation about what you are observing or feeling.

THOUGHTS FOR LEADERS

Often, a great performer will produce exceptionally well and interact positively with management but interact negatively with other employees. It's a kind of "kiss up, power down" scenario. People like this are friendly and cooperative with management but rude to subordinates or fellow workers.

- Become aware. Management may be unaware of the destructive nature of these individuals since it is easy to be blinded by the individual's high performance—or kiss-up style. Leaders need to create the perception of being a good listener. Perception is almost as important as the actual act of being a good listener. If people believe you are willing to listen, they will come to you. Bottom line is when they come to you, make them your priority, hold your calls, shut your door (if appropriate) give them your undivided attention. Great leaders listen and seek the honest opinions of employees from all levels of the organization. Don't rely on your direct subordinates to tell you the whole truth.

- Avoid choosing to *look the other way*.

- Be responsible to the team, the whole.

- Avoid making concessions to a hotshot in the canoe if the style of this person's performance is adversely impacting the performance of others—no exceptions, even if it's family or friends.

- Don't become a hostage to top performers.

- As a leader, it is a mistake to think that a person's productivity outweighs the adversity they create within the canoe.

- Control or remove *hotshots* or *prima donnas* if they are destructive to the whole. Their productivity cannot outweigh that of the entire canoe.

- Sit down with the prima donnas and ask them why they are putting themselves in jeopardy. Get below the surface of comments such as "the others are incompetent" and get to the real behavioral issue. If you are able to bring an individual like this back as a productive member of the canoe, you will then have the power of your entire team moving in concert. Until you address these individuals, you will be missing the real power of your organization. You have to be ready to let go. Otherwise, they can control you and the organization and will limit your success. If you listen with an open mind and don't create a win-lose conversation, most high-powered people will tell you they want to be part of something great. As the Canoe Theory says, if they aren't happy, they have the right to be happy ... and maybe they need to be on their own and not part of your team in order to be that way.

- Listen to the majority and relative volume of employee opinions to discover who in the canoe is missing the A + P = E *(Attitude + Performance = Employability)* application.

- Check in with someone you trust and verify you are not in the way of your people being successful. Your leadership will create the accepted culture of behavior, and everyone will model after your behavior. You've worked hard to become the leader, so make certain you walk the Canoe Theory talk if you want to create a long-lasting, resilient team.

THOUGHTS FOR ASSOCIATES

- Contribute to the canoe in a positive manner. Negativity is unacceptable.

- If you are a top performer, consider that along the way someone assisted you when you were an average paddler. Now that you have done well, do not lose your humility. (Otherwise, you might just get it back by being taken down a notch or two.)

- Paddle for the team. Meeting or surpassing a goal individually is great, but not if it comes at the expense of others. For example, if your paperwork isn't turned in and others can't do their jobs, you aren't participating as a team member but rather just paddling for one—yourself. The team matters—not pulling your weight is unacceptable.

- Realize that to be a professional means providing total cooperation. You will be admired and valued when you come from a place of achievement and cooperation, not from a place of achievement based on a self-focused attitude.

- Provide a positive, professional perspective and be willing to confront those who participate negatively in the canoe.

- Take responsibility to address negative situations in the canoe and attempt to create a positive change. For example, ask your Teammate (who you perceive is negative) out to lunch or to talk somewhere out of the office. Ask if he or she is *all right*. Asking a general question is a great way to open up an honest dialogue. Remember, it's essential that you come from an honest place of interest and support rather than from one of judgment or criticism.

- Be responsible for your own attitude. If you find yourself being negative and unable to shift your attitude, you have a choice: find out why you are feeling negative and resolve it or leave the canoe for one that makes you happy. If you stay, take the time to dig down and unearth why you are not happy. Typically, if you are miserable and can get to the root of your misery, you have a chance to change your view. In either case, you are required to remain supportive, not only for the sake of the canoe, but also for your own well-being.

- Remain positive. Spreading negativity is not the solution; If you do so, you will ultimately undermine the canoe and your own personal integrity.

THE BOTTOM LINE

Being a great paddler with outstanding results is only being half a professional; the other half is acting like one. Realize that no one is indispensable and that respect is based upon A + P = E *(Attitude + Performance = Employability)*. When you are a top performer, you have the responsibility to contribute to others' successes. Real top performers understand that when they are part of a team, the team matters as much, if not more, than the top performers. Supporting others and helping them achieve your level of accomplishment is a worthwhile objective.

If you can no longer support the canoe you have chosen, you should consider getting into a canoe you like. Remember however, if you don't like something in this canoe, you might very well find a similar situation in the next canoe.

Take a brave stand and realize that maintaining a positive attitude is a key component for the canoe's success.

If management doesn't have fair rules or treats people unequally, it's up to you to bring this to their attention. If they don't take a more balanced, fair approach, then you can choose to remove yourself from the canoe.

" Make it **happen**. "

TENET 6:

IN TIMES OF PERSONAL CRISIS, YOUR
COMPATRIOTS WILL PADDLE FOR YOU

The Canoe Theory accommodates crisis. If a member of the canoe has a death in the family, an illness, a health issue, or serious personal problems the canoe deems a crisis, the canoe will pull over to shore temporarily and allow the individual a reasonable period of time to solve the crisis while the other team members take up the paddling.

Personal lives and business lives are entwined; one affects the other. If an individual is experiencing a crisis or great personal difficulty, he or she needs to consider sharing the situation with a superior or the Human Resources department. This helps gain understanding for possible poor paddling during the crisis.

In most cases, a reasonable time away from the organization may support the member and resolve the issue.

Compassion is a great leadership virtue. At one time or another, everyone runs into a personal crisis. Nothing builds respect for management or teammates more than extending compassion in times of crisis. But, crisis isn't only an employee issue; it's a people issue. For a team to be a real team, compassion needs to go both ways. Beneath the title, leaders are people just like everyone else; they have real issues and personal lives that may take a toll on them.

A crisis may be anything that could completely take an individual's mind off the job at hand—paddling. Examples include:

•   A death in the family or near the family circle

•   Alcohol or drug abuse correction (consult your policy and procedures manual to make sure your actions coincide with federal and state law)

- An emotional crisis

- Physical injury

- Financial crisis

- A natural disaster such as a hurricane, flood, or earthquake (listen with compassion, probe as deeply as Human Resources will allow, and as deeply as the employee feels comfortable sharing)

THOUGHTS FOR LEADERS

- Foster an environment of trust and confidentiality among the team.

- Be in tune with your employees so you can recognize when an individual is experiencing problems. Be alert and be aware. If you aren't meeting daily with your employees, even briefly, you may not be alert to subtle changes that may indicate that something's up. If you become as tuned in with your employees as you might be with a major client, you will be surprised how much you will learn about your team members and their struggles.

- Let the team know, in a manner both general and confidential, that a team member is experiencing a personal difficulty and that the team should expect less from this person for a short period of time (see Human Resources before you share, even if the employee approves). This sharing helps create a hedge against speculation, rumors, and resentment in the canoe.

- When helping the troubled employee, leaders should ensure that they are not acting in a manner that will result in employee litigation. Again, Human Resources should always be consulted. There are other concerns to be aware of in such a situation in addition to legal issues, such as decreased morale, employee distrust, and diminished perceived authority.

- Agree upon a reasonable time for correction. Remind the employee that his or her compatriots will take up the paddling during that time.

THOUGHTS FOR ASSOCIATES

- Be sensitive to your teammates' issues. It would be great if everyone had to walk in the shoes of another before they made judgments.

- Act like a leader and support your teammate, supervisor, or leader in time of need. View this as an opportunity to support the whole and take a positive approach with a solution that serves everyone.

- Be willing to use open dialogue in difficult or stressful times. If your work load becomes overwhelming because you are being supportive to a co-worker in crisis, communicate with your supervisor so you can create balance or develop an action plan to relieve your stress. Being supportive of a fellow employee is critical, but that support should not come at the expense of overwhelming yourself.

- Let management know if something is beginning to influence your performance in the canoe.

- Seek outside help when a crisis presents itself, or discuss the crisis with your organization's Human Resources department or with your supervisor.

- Be accountable for developing and following your own plan for recovery.

- Solve your problem within a reasonable amount of time as established by a mutual agreement with management.

THE BOTTOM LINE

The best canoes are those with a foundation of trust, understanding, and cooperation. Canoes with members who share the core value of teamwork will always take up the slack for those in crisis because they understand that the team's responsibilities are their responsibilities. Temporary release from the canoe should be in line with Human Resources and legal guidelines. Compassion builds powerful canoes.

Employees, in turn, must realize that organizations also experience crises. At times the company needs a bit of compassion or understanding. The organization may not have the ability to provide all the resources necessary due to financial constraints.

As a result, the employee must exhibit understanding and allow the canoe to take time to regroup. This will require the employee to paddle more assertively until the canoe has time to resolve the crisis it is experiencing. And everyone must understand the crisis, for the crisis should only exist for a reasonable amount of time.

Everyone has the right to expect that the canoe will have a plan to get out of the crisis. It is your responsibility to ask questions and make intelligent, informed decisions. If the canoe isn't moving toward more stable waters, you have the right to find a canoe that can support you and your family.

TENET 7:
YOU HAVE THE RIGHT TO BE HAPPY

The Canoe Theory includes the belief that everyone has a fundamental right to be happy. If individuals put themselves at risk in the canoe, they can't be happy. Why would people want to stay in a canoe if they aren't happy? This means if a member of the canoe doesn't like the paddle, where he or she sits, where the canoe is going, who leads the canoe, or anything at all, that person has a right to leave and find a canoe that is better suited.

It's a matter of choice. But some people have circumstances beyond their control or believe they don't have options. Most people would agree their life isn't always how they've designed it. There are difficulties, tragedies, poor decisions, and unpleasant circumstances. But one thing that no one can take from a person is the way that he or she looks at those circumstances. This is the significant distinction of the Canoe Theory: being happy is a state of mind. And the core of this state of mind is under our control. It is appreciation and gratitude.

The Canoe Theory maintains that if an individual member in the canoe is not happy for any reason, the canoe will simply pull over to shore and let that individual out so he or she can get into a canoe that promises greater satisfaction.

Life is too complex and too short to be in a canoe you are not comfortable with. Everyone in an organization must realize that being in any canoe is a choice.

THOUGHTS FOR LEADERS

- Be in touch with your people. You need to be able to identify the speed and direction of the canoe and the individuals in it.

Changes in an individual's contribution may directly reflect his or her satisfaction with the canoe, or it may indicate that the individual is in crisis.

- Recognize, support, and monitor the contribution of team members.

- Create an environment of trust and openness.

- Seek out new ideas and new ways of doing business from everyone in the canoe. People whose ideas are asked for have a higher rate of job satisfaction.

- Be a compassionate listener. Leading your canoe requires compassion; if an individual is not happy in the canoe, it will generally show in attitude or performance. If an individual is not happy, it may not always be about the canoe. Your discovery process with the individual may require you to look deeper. If you listen carefully to the issue, you may discover what is really going on.

- Focus on the employee. If the employee isn't happy and you believe you have done all that is possible, it may be time to assist the individual by discussing the option of seeking another canoe. This may occur during a frank and compassionate conversation where you talk with the employee about what he or she is looking for in a canoe, and whether that can be found in your organization.

- Consider that termination can often be a gift that gives new opportunities to an individual. Be very aware that the employee may not necessarily perceive it as such at first. One very effective way to consider termination is to ask for their resignation, this is after you consult your Human Resources department or your employee handbook to be aware of the process your organization has in place. Typically a calm, honest, and candid conversation with the person is very effective. In most cases, if someone is not performing well; typically it is a training issue, personal crisis situation, or attitude problem. A training issue can be handled, a personal crisis can be understood, but an attitude problem is a choice and when someone chooses a negative attitude, typically it is an indication, they are not happy. If you can get that person to realize how they are perceived, while telling them—it's okay you want them to be happy, you have a chance at having them remove themselves.

THOUGHTS FOR ASSOCIATES

- Monitor your own behavior as a member of the canoe.

- Don't be a victim—the power of choice is yours. In life or in work, sometimes you may feel as if you are powerless or don't have a choice. This is not true. Even those perceived as powerless have the choice of accepting their situation as it is or taking all available means to change things. Sometimes this is not easy, as when your resources are limited or the choice of suitable canoes is slim. But every waking moment of your life, you retain the choice to accept things as they are or change them for the better. (For further inspiration, refer to the quotation from Dr. Martin Luther King Jr. at the end of Tenet #6 or look at W. Mitchell's web site http://www.wmitchell.com.)

- Speak up. The choice to be part of something does not mean abdicating thoughts and ideas; it means being committed to being successful and contributing, not being complacent and robotic. Remember to use the canoe's rights and responsibilities to support your conversations with your supervisor or leader.

- Take a risk and share ideas and thoughts to make the canoe a better place.

- Evaluate your situation. Staying in a canoe that is not a good fit only leads to frustration, resentment, and poor performance— the end result may be that you will become disgruntled or your employment may be terminated. If you are not happy with the canoe you are in for any reason, find one where you can be happy, or build a canoe of your own.

- Realize that if you are not happy, there will always be a canoe that will provide a better fit. It is your responsibility to have the courage to find a canoe that is right for you.

- Be open to the possibility that staying in a canoe where you are unhappy is more painful than having the courage to seek out a new one.

- If you decide to stay in the canoe despite the fact that you are unhappy, you need to have the integrity to support leadership and the canoe.

- Practice integrity. Gossip, negativity, and passive-aggressive behavior demonstrate a lack of integrity. Integrity is a personal trait, without which one is never able to pursue quality results for the team.

- Make the choice. Get fully in the canoe or choose a different one.

FINAL THOUGHTS

The Canoe Theory is all about choice. You have the power to choose the canoe you want to paddle in. When you choose to be in a canoe, be in the canoe 100%.

The value of being in the canoe 100% is the win you can create for yourself and for the canoe. Winning teams talk about achieving through the efforts of a group of committed individuals.

Once you've made the commitment, take on a new level of responsibility or be a contributor in some way that supports both the organization's success and your own. Take the time to find your passion and purpose, the reason you are in the canoe, and consider the winning outcome you will achieve if you stay in. This is a very personal decision that only you can make.

Remember that one person can make a positive difference, and you don't need to own the company to be that person. When an individual stands for positive change, he or she can make a significant contribution to a department, a team, or the entire company.

When you bring in a new teammate, make certain the new team member knows he or she is expected to contribute thoughts and ideas— even if they are contrary to what is presently in place. New ideas are the energy for development and growth in any entity. Stirring them up is good energy. However, once a decision is made, everyone needs to get behind that choice or chosen direction.

No one should be in a canoe he or she is unhappy with. Being in a canoe that represents a wrong fit leads to underperformance, frustration, and ultimately, a negative attitude. Staying in a canoe that is wrong for an individual is a matter of choice. Every individual needs to take full accountability for continuing that choice.

When an employee wants to leave the canoe but can't for some reason, he or she needs to have the integrity to maintain a positive attitude and paddle with 100% effort until another, more suitable canoe is found.

It is everyone's responsibility to take on a negative paddler. Those who gossip should be challenged, for those who do not challenge this behavior demonstrate the same lack of integrity as the gossipers themselves.

When you listen to gossip and negativity but remain quiet, that behavior is often considered complicities. Be courageous enough to take a stand.

THE MORAL OF THE CANOE THEORY

If you are going to be in the canoe, then support the canoe or have the integrity to leave rather than stay and undermine the canoe.

Make the choice—be happy. Support the direction, the team members, the leadership, and the philosophy of the canoe. Traveling in a canoe takes skill, balance, and coordination to navigate successfully to a specific destination. This is the essence of the Canoe Theory. Balance and coordination are critical to making the journey the best experience possible.

If you cannot support the canoe for any reason, then fight for the change you believe is important. Speak up, even if what you're saying is not popular. If that change is not possible and you decide to stay in the canoe, then have the integrity to avoid gossip, negativity, or anything that undermines the canoe.

If you are unable to maintain a positive attitude and paddle with the spirit of complete commitment, then have the integrity to leave the canoe.

The option of staying in the canoe and undermining its integrity should not be considered an acceptable option. If you're going to be in the canoe, then be completely in the canoe.

There's a great quotation that says, "We make a difference—if we choose!" Behind this statement is a well-known story:

One day a man was walking along the beach when he noticed a figure in the distance. As he got closer, he realized the figure was that of a boy picking something up and gently throwing it into the ocean.

Approaching the boy, he asked, "What are you doing?" The youth replied, "Throwing a starfish into the ocean. The sun is up and the tide is going out. If I don't throw them back, they'll die."

"Son," the man said, "don't you realize there are miles and miles of beach and hundreds of starfish? You can't possibly make a difference!"

After listening politely, the boy bent down, picked up another starfish, and threw it into the surf. Then, smiling at the man, he said, "I made a difference for that one."

Adapted from *The Star Thrower* by Loren Eisely

We all make a difference in one way or another.

What about you and the canoe you are in? Are you making a difference? Are you just riding in the canoe or are you contributing? Are you vested in yourself and the direction of the canoe or are you just taking up a seat?

One person can make a difference. It often takes only small contributions to make big strides.

So, you choose to pick up your paddle and dig in or, to enact tenet # 7, "You have the right to be happy" and find a canoe you like. The choice is yours.

Many of our readers and attendees of our conferences know that English is no longer the sole international language of business. We firmly believe that the concepts presented in The Canoe Theory are not bound by geography or culture. For that reason, we have also provided the central tenets of The Canoe Theory in Spanish.

"Intention
is everything."

Una Introducción a La Teoría
de la Canoa para los lectores
de habla hispana.

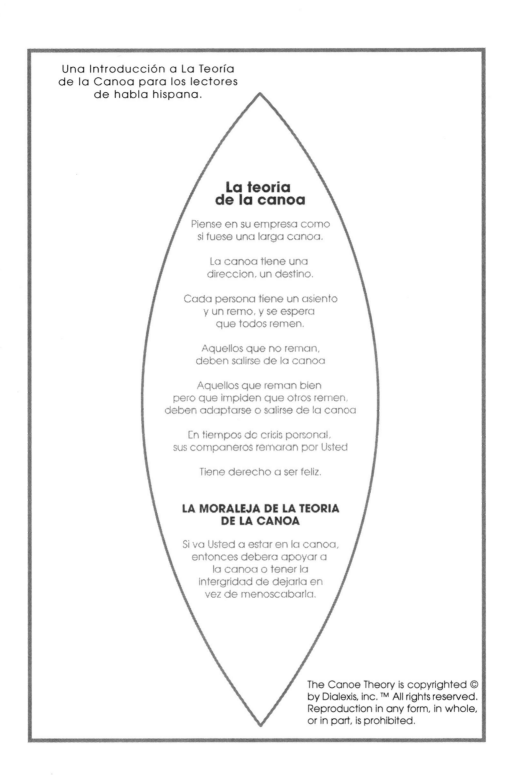

La teoria
de la canoa

Piense en su empresa como
si fuese una larga canoa.

La canoa tiene una
direccion, un destino.

Cada persona tiene un asiento
y un remo, y se espera
que todos remen.

Aquellos que no reman,
deben salirse de la canoa

Aquellos que reman bien
pero que impiden que otros remen,
deben adaptarse o salirse de la canoa

En tiempos de crisis porsonal,
sus companeros remaran por Usted

Tiene derecho a ser feliz.

LA MORALEJA DE LA TEORIA
DE LA CANOA

Si va Usted a estar en la canoa,
entonces debera apoyar a
la canoa o tener la
intergridad de dejarla en
vez de menoscabarla.

La Teoría de la Canoa

Principio 1: Piense en su empresa como si fuese una larga canoa

*   ¿A qué clase de canoa desea pertenecer?

*   Conozca la cultura de su empresa—considere los diversos esti-
        los de comportamiento dentro de su Canoa.

*   Cada persona llega a la canoa con sus propios principios y cre-
        encias; cada individuo tiene sus antecedentes; ¿Cómo unir a
        un grupo compuesto de individuos con diferentes experiencias
        para lograr un éxito común?

Principio 2: La canoa tiene una dirección, un destino

*   Una Causa impacta más que una Misión o una Meta ~
        Identifíquese con La Causa.

*   Comprenda cuál es su bandera personal y enlácela al éxito de
        la empresa.

*   Comparta su bandera o el curso que usted desea seguir con su
        equipo gerencial.

Principio 3: Cada persona tiene un asiento y un remo, y se espera que
            todos remen

*   Puede ser necesario que todos se sienten dónde quepan.

- Hágase 100% responsable de todo aquello a lo que se compromete.

- Para remar con excelencia usted debe satisfacer todas las expectativas.

Principio 4: Aquellos que no reman, deben salirse de la canoa

- A nadie le agrada ver a otra persona al otro extremo de la canoa y preguntarse ¿por qué sigue con la Empresa una persona que no rema?

Principio 5: Aquellos que reman bien pero que impiden que otros remen, deben adaptarse o salirse de la canoa

- A + D = E (Actitud + Desempeño = Empleo).

- Tenga el valor para dar todo su apoyo al grupo o de lo contrario salir de la canoa.

Principio 6: En tiempos de crisis personal, sus compañeros remarán por Usted (por un período de tiempo razonable, para darle tiempo a adaptarse)

- Comunique con el equipo gerencial acerca de la crisis que le enfrenta; determine, de manera justa, lo que será un "periodo razonable de tiempo" durante el cuál usted puede resolver la crisis.

•   La comprensión incluye la ayuda mutua.
         (Las empresas también enfrentan situaciones
         difíciles que requieren la comprensión de todos).

Principio 7: Tiene derecho a ser feliz. (Si hay algo de la canoa que le
         desagrada, la canoa se acercara a la costa para permitirle
         a Usted el subirse a una canoa que sea de su agrado)

•   A dónde sea que se dirige, allí se encuentra.

•   Indague hacia adentro de sí mismo.

•   Usted debe elegir entre estar dentro o fuera de la canoa ~
         comprométase a lograr su felicidad.

La Moraleja de la Teoría de la Canoa

Si va Usted a estar en la canoa, entonces debera apoyar a la canoa o
tener la integridad de dejarla en vez de menoscabarla

PART
four

The Canoe Theory:
Implementation

IDEAS TO KEEP YOUR TEAM PADDLING

Here are some ways to keep the Canoe Theory moving and working in your organization:

- Buy a canoe, cut it lengthwise, and mount half of it on the office wall. For offices with space, hang a whole canoe from the ceiling.

- Create a team paddle with an inscription that reads "Top Paddler" and rotate it quarterly to the group you believe exemplifies the most effective teamwork.

- Create the rights and responsibilities that support the culture and direction of your canoe. Distribute them to all team members and post where appropriate.

- Take a photo of teams and departments holding paddles and place it in the lunchroom or reception area.

- Each month, recognize the best paddlers.

- Present a Best Paddler Award annually.

- Etch the key tenets of the Canoe Theory on a plaque.

- Send edible chocolate canoes to customers and business partners.

- Integrate the Canoe Theory in your policies and procedures manuals.

- Focus on one Canoe Theory tenet per month.

- Create a fun event for the organization (bowling, softball, picnic, etc.). It is essential to get to know each other.

- Print a Canoe Theory tenet on T-shirts and hand out the shirts at company events.

Keep the Canoe Theory alive by referencing it daily. the Canoe Theory provides a simple, effective way to communicate and will become the new culture of your organization.

Thank you to all of the employees and leaders who have shared their stories. What we have ultimately learned is that we are all in this together. The more we focus on others and support one another, the stronger and more proficient we become.

The Canoe Theory is dedicated to everyone who takes a courageous stand for a better, more cohesive work environment.

Share with us what you've done to integrate the Canoe Theory into your organization. Let us know how we can support you as you build and paddle your canoe.

Dialexis, inc.™

1-800-98PROFIT
(1-800-987-7694)

www.dialexis.com

THE CANOE'S RESOURCE LIBRARY

Every canoe needs a collection of resources on board to assist in the continuous improvement of all dimensions of the effectiveness, efficiency, and growth of each team member.

These resources should be placed in the front of the canoe so that the paddlers may consider and refer to them before encountering any white-water rapids.

Resources can include books, trade publications, planned activities, training sessions, and many other forms of creative or productive tools.

The library must be updated frequently so that old and overused concepts and resources are jettisoned and replaced with fresh ideas and strategies.

The following resources are good starting points, but each canoe should build its own library.

SUGGESTED PUBLICATIONS

Fast Company
(www.fastcompany.com)

Harvard Business Review
(www.harvardbusinessonline.org)

Business 2-0
(www.business2.com)

Wired
(www.wired.com)

SUGGESTED READING FOR THE CANOE:

Lightning in a Bottle: Proven Lessons for Leading Change
Baum, David
Chicago: Dearborn, a Kaplan Professional Company, 2000

Leaders: Strategies for Taking Charge
Bennis, Warren, and Burt Nanus
New York: Harper Business, 2nd Ed., 1997

Self-Leadership and the One Minute Manager
Blanchard, Ken, Fowler, Susan and Hawkins, Laurence
New York: William Morrow and Company, Inc., 2005

The One Minute Apology: A Powerful Way to Make Things Better
Blanchard, Ken and Margret McBride
New York: William Morrow and Company, Inc., 2003

The Secret: What Great Leaders Know—And Do
Blanchard, Ken and Mark Miller
San Francisco: Berrett-Koehler Pubishers, Inc., 2004

Don't Sweat the Small Stuff At Work
Carlson, Richard
New York: Hyperion, 1998

Management 21C
Chowdhury, Subir
London: Financial Times Prentice-Hall, 2000

Managing In a Time of Great Change
Drucker, Peter F.
New York: Truman Talley Books/Plume 1998

Adventures of a Bystander
Drucker, Peter F.
New York: John Wiley & Sons, Inc. 1994

Management Challenges for the 21st Century
Drucker, Peter F.
New York: Harper Business, 1999

On the Profession of Management
Drucker, Peter F.
Boston: Harvard Business School Press, 1998

The World Is Flat: A Brief History of the 21st Century
Friedman, Thomas L.
New York: Farrar, Straus, and Giroux, 2005

On Leadership
Gardner, John
New York: The Free Press, 1990

Customer Satisfaction Is Worthless, Customer Loyalty Is Priceless
Gitomer, Jeffery
Austin: Bard press, 1998

The Talent Solution: Aligning Strategy and People to Achieve Extraordinary Results
Gubman, Edward L.
New York: McGraw-Hill, 1998

The Age of Paradox
Handy, Charles
Boston: The Harvard Business School Press, 1994

The Age of Unreason
Handy, Charles
Boston: The Harvard Business School Press, 1989

Beyond Certainty
Handy, Charles
Boston: The Harvard Business School Press, 1996

Finding and Keeping Good employees
Harris, Jim and Joan Brannick
AMACON, 1999

Six Sigma
Harry, Mikel and Richard Schroeder
New York: Currency Doubleday, 2000

On Managing People
Harvard Business Review
Boston: The Harvard Business School Press, 1999

Leading Beyond the Walls
Hesselbein, Frances, et.al.
San Francisco: Jossey-Bass Publishers, 1999

The Service Profit Chain
Heskett, James L., et. al.
New York: The Free Press, 1997

Leader to Leader
Hesselbein, Frances and Paul Cowen, eds, The Drucker Foundation
San Francisco: Jossey-Bass Publishers, 1999

Leaders of the Future
Hesselbein, Frances and Paul Cowen, eds., The Drucker Foundation
San Francisco: Jossey-Bass Publishers, 1996

Who Moved My Cheese?
Johnson, Spencer
New York: G.P. Putnam's Sons, 1998

E-Volve! Succeeding in the Digital Culture of Tomorrow
Kanter, Rosabeth-Moss
Boston: Harvard Business School Press, 2001

The Balanced Scorecard
Kaplan, Robert S. and David P. Norton
Boston: Harvard Business School Press, 1996

The Monk and the Riddle
Komisar, Randy
Boston: Harvard Business School Press, 2000

Leading Change
Kotter, John P.
Boston: Harvard Business School Press, 1996

The Five Dysfunctions of a Team: A Leadership Fable
Lencioni, Patrick
San Francisco: Jossey-Bass, A Wiley Company, 2002

Fish: A Remarkable Way to Boost Morale and Improve Profits
Lundin, Stephen C., Paul, Harry and Christensen, John
New York: Hyperion, 2000

Fish Tales: Real-Life Stories to Help You Transform Your Workplace and Your Life
Lundin, Stephen C., Christensen, John and Paul, Harry
New York: Hyperion, 2002

The Horizontal Organization
Ostroff, Frank
New York: Oxford University Press, 1999

The Human Equation: Building Profits by Putting People First
Pfeffer, Jeffrey
Boston: Harvard University Press, 1998

The New Paradigm in Business
Ray, Michael and Alan Rinzle
New York: G.P. Putnam's Sons, 1993

The Leaders Handbook: Making Things Happen, Getting Things Done
Scholtes, Peter R.
New York: McGraw-Hill, 1998

The Team Handbook: How to Use Teams to Improve Quality
Scholtes, Peter R., et.al.
Madison: Joiner associates, Inc., 1998

The Dance of Change
Senge, Peter M.
New York: Currency-Doubleday, 1999

The Fifth Discipline: The Art and Practice of the Learning Organization
Senge, Peter M.
New York: Currency-Doubleday, 1990

The Fifth Discipline Fieldbook: Strategies and Tools for Building a Learning
Organization
Senge, Peter M.,et.al.
New York: Currency-Doubleday, 1994

The Great Game of Business
Stack, Jack
New York: Currency-Doubleday, 1992

In Search of Solutions: 60 Ways to Guide Your Problem-Solving Group
Quinlivan-Hall, David and Peter Renner
Amsterdam: Pfeiffer & Company, 1994

Generations At Work
Zemke, Ron, Raines, Claire and Filipczak, Bob
New York: AMACOM, 2000

TO CONTACT THE AUTHORS

For information about our products, contact us at

Dialexis, inc.™

1-800-98-PROFIT (800-987-7634)

Visit us at www.dialexis.com to learn more about how to implement the
Canoe Theory in your organization and to obtain information about
other programs and publications developed by Dialexis, inc.™

Lightning Source UK Ltd.
Milton Keynes UK

171847UK00002B/1/P